THE FATHER YOU'VE BEEN WAITING FOR

THE FATHER YOU'VE BEEN WAITING FOR

Portrait of a Perfect Dad

MARK STIBBE

FOREWORD BY DIANE LOUISE JORDAN

Authentic

MILTON KEYNES ● COLORADO SPRINGS ● HYDERABAD

Authentic Media, 9 Holdom Avenue, Bletchley, Milton Keynes, Bucks.,
MK1 1QR
1820 Jet Stream Drive, Colorado Springs, CO 80921, USA
OM Authentic Media, Medchal Road, Jeedimetla Village, Secunderabad
500 055, A.P., India
www.authenticmedia.co.uk
Authentic Media is a division of IBS-STL U.K., limited by guarantee, with
its registered office at Kingstown Broadway, Carlisle, Cumbria CA3 0HA.
Registered in England & Wales No.1216232. Registered charity 270162

British Library Cataloguing in Publication Data
A catalogue record for this book is available from the British Library.

ISBN 978-1-86024-593-0

Cover image by Charlie Mackesey
Cover design by Peter Barnsley
Print Management by Adare Carwin
Printed and bound by J.H. Haynes and Co Ltd., Sparkford

To my beloved daughter, Hannah.

CONTENTS

ACKNOWLEDGEMENTS

I am very grateful to Malcolm Down and the people at Authentic Media for all the work they've done and for publishing this book.

I must confess my debt to the work of Middle East expert Kenneth Bailey, whose books on the prodigal son (especially *Poet and Peasant* and *The Cross and the Prodigal*) have helped me to see the parable as Jesus would have intended it – from within the cultural context of his original audience.

I am also grateful to artist Charlie Mackesey for allowing me to use his amazing painting on the cover of this book. Thank you, Charlie.

I am indebted to my friend Barry Adams for allowing us to use 'Father's Love Letter' at the end of Chapter 8. For more information on this, see www.fathersloveletter.com.

I am grateful to Zondervan publishers for allowing me to reproduce in the epilogue the quite beautiful retelling of the parable by the writer Philip Yancey. Yancey's story was originally published in his best-selling book, *What's so Amazing about Grace?*

I am grateful to those who have shared their stories in this book. Their names are either not included or changed in most cases. These stories are incredibly personal and I am keen to protect the anonymity of all concerned.

I am grateful to the publishers of the New Living Translation of the Bible – the version most quoted and used in this book.

I am grateful to those who have read the manuscript of this book and made invaluable comments, especially Andy Carpenter.

And finally, I am grateful to my Heavenly Father for his love and inspiration.

FOREWORD

I'll never forget that Saturday morning when I opened up a national newspaper to read a double page spread about the highly successful life and career of Diane Louise Jordan. I'll never forget the surge of emptiness and remorse that filled me as I read about my enviable lifestyle. Here was an article about me, all the details were correct and yet what I read didn't match how I felt. Despite success beyond my wildest dreams, I didn't feel satisfied. In fact, as my success grew, so did my despair.

Recently I was watching a programme about a highly successful businessman who'd taken a 'gap' year to find 'what he was looking for'. He returned, challenged and refreshed but still yearning for that something to make him complete.

A young friend of mine who seems blessed with everything – intelligence, charm, good looks, popularity, health and much more – lives most days feeling 'desperately wrong'.

So many of us, from various walks of life, even those who've tasted success, who've achieved lifetime ambitions, who've had the best of everything, have never satisfied that hunger at the core of our being.

Many of us crave to be understood, to be accepted, to be valued, to have purpose. We search for this fulfilment in a variety of ways. It might be through power, status, achievement, relationship, addiction. For some, this can be a lifelong unfulfilling, unquenchable quest.

I believed I could fulfil my hunger through career and material success – that was my dream.

I'd spent most of my life believing I had the ability to fulfil my destiny. And my most frightening realisation came on that Saturday morning reading the newspaper article. I'd played my best hand and had still lost. Success alone wasn't the answer. It was only when I'd run out of answers that, in desperation, I decided to let God have a go.

It's the best decision I've ever made.

If, like me, you're convinced there must be more to life; if, like me, you've experienced the yearning for something else; if, like me, you're desperate to purge the emptiness, then this book may well help. Maybe the nudge in you isn't a full-blown craving but mere curiosity. This is still for you.

Today, more than ever, we have an insatiable spiritual hunger, and in this timely book Mark Stibbe believes he has the answer. The answer to the meaning of life; the answer to the hunger for total fulfilment. The answer, Mark believes, is the Father love of God because God is the purpose and a relationship with Him is the key to significant living. Mark passionately believes that the love of God fills the gap.

Foreword

In this accessible, thoughtful book, packed with an abundance of relevant, faith-warming anecdotes, and biblical evidence, Mark Stibbe exposes and explores the nature of God by highlighting ten aspects of his character. The God he reveals isn't a divine bully, who punishes us for wrong-doing, but rather one full of compassion and love, who promises a relationship that will satisfy – a relationship built on such solid foundations that we will never need to doubt our worth and purpose again.

If you are searching for answers, if you are yearning for wholeness, if you are interested in exploring the meaning of life and/or the relevance of the God of the Bible in the twenty-first century, then Mark's book is definitely worth a read. In fact, this is a must-read for anyone who wants a direct, honest explanation of how the remarkable God who created the universe and more, loves and is interested in an exclusive, intimate, life-transforming relationship with you. Who knows, it may well contribute to changing your life – forever!

Diane Louise Jordan

THE PORTRAIT OF A PERFECT DAD

I never knew my father. In fact, I have never even known his name. Several months before my twin and I were born, he decided to leave my birth mother and abandoned her to fend for herself. All this put such a burden on my mother that she gave us up for adoption. Having spent the first seven months of our lives in an orphanage, my twin sister and I were then adopted into a new family.

It is hard to assess how deep the father wound goes in my life. Even though my relationship with my adoptive father was excellent, there was always a love hunger or, more specifically, 'a father hunger' in my heart. For decades, this emotional cavity left me with a deep-seated sense of abandonment and an intense fear of separation. It has taken me many years to find healing for this great ache in my heart. The journey has been long, arduous and, at times, painful. But in the end I can definitely say that it has been infinitely worthwhile.

THE FATHER-SHAPED HOLE

It has been said that today's generation of young people – those in the 14–35 age bracket – are the generation of divorced parents, absent fathers and broken homes. More than any other in history, this generation is the 'fatherless generation'.

The trend towards fatherlessness is not brand new. It has, in fact, been building and growing since the Second World War. Novelist Ernest Hemingway's life is evidence of this. Hemingway was very close to his father Ed, who eventually killed himself in 1928. Hemingway missed his father desperately, yet at the same time he blamed him for committing suicide. Hemingway took on the nickname 'Papa', which he used till his life ended (also by his own hand) in 1961. Hemingway used this name because he wanted to become the ideal father he felt his dad had not been.

At the beginning of one of his short stories, Hemingway makes reference to the tale of a Spanish father who wanted to be reconciled with his son, who had run away from home to the city of Madrid. The father missed the son and put an advert in the local newspaper, *El Liberal*. The advertisement read, 'Paco, meet me at the Hotel Montana at noon on Tuesday. All is forgiven! Love, Papa.'

When the father went to the Hotel Montana the next day at noon there were eight hundred young men named Paco waiting for their fathers.

Although this is fiction, here again we see evidence of the 'father-shaped hole' that exists in so many people in the west today. There are literally millions of teenagers and young adults who have never known the unconditional, pure, consistent and affectionate love of a dad. And the consequences have been quite devastating.

WHEN FATHERS ARE ABSENT

The consequences are, first of all, devastating *socially*. In society there is no question that we are now reaping a whirlwind because of decades of absentee fathers. In the UK, approximately one in six fathers is no longer actually living with his children. Approximately 8 per cent of all birth certificates in Britain do not reveal the identity of the child's father.

Everywhere we are confronted by evidence of the social results of fatherlessness. A friend of mine who works for the BBC recently had to give an after-dinner speech. He found himself sitting next to a senior criminologist at Cambridge University. In conversation she told him that any assessment of the driving factors of teenage criminality and prison sentences threw up three key statistics:

- Roughly 60 per cent are typical school failures, with poor reading and low education skills.
- Roughly 70 per cent are on drugs and part of the underworld drugs fraternity by supply or usage.

- Roughly 80 per cent have grown up without a father and
  carry the deepest scar of failure and rejection – the
  absence of secure, responsible commitment.

When Margaret Thatcher was Prime Minister, one of the
many things she did was to begin work on the creation of a
Child Support Agency. What was it that drove her to do
that? It was when she went to a nativity play and met a child
who said, 'I don't want my dad coming to this, 'cos I'll stand
out, 'cos nobody else has got a dad who's coming.'

The consequences of fatherlessness have been devastating
socially. They have also been devastating *spiritually*. It has been
said that the cry of the current generation is, 'Will you always
be there for me?' Why is this? The answer is simple. It is
because so many teenagers and adults have experienced
abandonment and rejection, particularly by their fathers. This
has produced a void in their lives that is far more than just
emotional and relational. It is spiritual too. Young people –
and not so young people – are longing spiritually for someone
to be for them what their dads were not. They are longing for
a father who will never leave nor forsake them, who will
always be there for them and who can always be trusted.

FATHER, WHERE IS THE LOVE?

Deep down, the biggest spiritual need of our day is for
intimacy, for the experience of loving and being loved. The

spiritual awakening happening in our culture today shows that many are looking for this need to be met through more than human relationships. People are looking for connection with the transcendent and the divine. Like Mulder and Scully in *The X Files*, they know 'the truth is out there' and they are declaring, 'I want to believe.' While they avoid institutional avenues, such people are certainly exploring less formal and familiar routes towards God. Desperate for contact with a more permanent and trustworthy father, they are on a spiritual quest as no other generation before them.

Again, the evidence for this search for the father is all around us. Look at contemporary pop music. In 2003, the hit single that was No. 1 in the UK charts for the longest time was a song by the Black Eyed Peas called 'Where is the Love?' The video of this single showed people questioning why injustice, poverty and hatred are rife in the world and crying out to God, 'Father, father, father, where is the love?' If this isn't the cry of today's generation, I don't know what is. As the song goes, 'Send us some guidance from above.'

Another pop single from 2004, this time by Anastacia, sends a similar message. Her song 'Left Alone Outside' was No. 1 in the European charts for weeks. It paints a poignant picture of the sense of isolation rampant among today's young people. Anastacia sings that she has been waiting all her life for a fairytale to come her way, but it hasn't happened. The romance hasn't blossomed, and the much-needed love hasn't materialised. So she finally concludes, 'I need to pray,' adding, 'Heavenly Father, please save me.'

THERE IS GOOD NEWS AFTER ALL

But all is not lost. I am writing this book to share with you some good news, and it's from my own personal experience, not from second-hand opinion. The good news is that there is a perfect Father we can all have access to and, more than that, a meaningful relationship with. I have known this dad for over twenty years now and he has never let me down, he's always been there for me, and above all he's filled the father-shaped hole in my soul.

So who is this dad? What is he really like? And how can I get to know him?

The answer is to be found in the pages of the Gospels, in the New Testament part of the Bible. In these four Gospels (the word 'gospel' means 'good news') we meet the most amazing human being who has ever lived, Jesus of Nazareth. I believe Jesus Christ was born to tell us that God is a perfect Father and we can have an eternal friendship with him. He was born to restore intimacy between us and our Father in heaven.

In this book I want to describe this Heavenly Father to you.

In order to do that, I am going to use one passage from the Bible. You can find it in Luke's Gospel, chapter 15, where, two thousand years ago, Jesus of Nazareth tells one of the best-loved stories of all time – the story of the prodigal son. This story is a parable; it is a Jewish form of storytelling in which a down-to-earth tale is used to illustrate a deep spiritual truth. The parable in Luke 15 – like all parables – has two levels. On the superficial level it tells the story of a son who said 'Drop dead!' to his father, ran away from home, and came back to find his dad waiting for him with arms opened wide. On the deeper level, it paints a picture of what human beings have done in running away from God, and how God has run to us in love.

I know no other story like this story, and you can find a version of it in the prologue to this book. In the pages that follow I am going to share simple observations about the father in the parable. These are all positive, heart-warming qualities that will stir your soul. But each of these qualities refers not just to the boy's dad but also, beyond that, to the one whom Jesus called 'our Father in heaven'. That's the deeper meaning of the parable and we will be excavating that level together.

In all of this I shall be proposing that it is really the dad who is the focus of the parable, not the son, and that this dad is quite simply amazing. I don't think I have ever met such a loving father as this. He is perfect in every way. And Jesus, I am convinced, was saying, 'Look at this father. . . . He is like my Father and your Father in heaven.'

In this book we will examine ten things that are noteworthy about the dad in this story. And I will show how each of these applies to God himself. Whatever image of God you have, prepare for it to be challenged and changed by what you about to read.

This is truly the Father you've been waiting for!

THE STORY OF
A LOVING FATHER

There was once a man who had two sons. The younger said to his father, 'Father, I want right now what's coming to me.'

So the father divided the property between them. It wasn't long before the younger son packed his bags and left for a distant country. There, undisciplined and dissolute, he wasted everything he had. After he had gone through all his money, there was a bad famine throughout that country and he began to suffer. He signed on with a citizen there who assigned him to his fields to feed the pigs. He was so hungry he would have eaten the corncobs in the pig slop, but no one would give him any.

That brought him to his senses. He said, 'All those farmhands working for my father sit down to three meals a day, and here I am starving to death. I'm going back to my father. I'll say to him, Father, I've sinned against God, I've sinned before you; I don't deserve to be called your son. Take me on as a hired hand.' He got right up and went home to his father.

When he was still a long way off, his father saw him. His heart pounding, he ran out, embraced him and kissed him. The son started his speech: 'Father, I've sinned against God, I've sinned before you; I don't deserve to be called your son ever again.'

But the father wasn't listening. He was calling to the servants, 'Quick. Bring a clean set of clothes and dress him. Put the family ring on his finger and sandals on his feet. Then get a grain-fed heifer and roast it. We're going to feast! We're going to have a wonderful time! My son is here – given up for dead and now alive! Given up for lost and now found!' And they began to have a wonderful time.

All this time, his older son was out in the field. When the day's work was done he came in. As he approached the house, he heard the music and dancing. Calling over one of the houseboys, he asked what was going on. The boy told him, 'Your brother came home. Your father has ordered a feast – barbecued beef! – because he has him home safe and sound.'

The older brother stalked off in an angry sulk and refused to join in. His father came out and tried to talk to him, but he wouldn't listen. The son said, 'Look how many years I've stayed here serving you, never giving you one moment of grief. But have you ever thrown a party for me and my friends? Then this son of yours who has thrown away your money on whores shows up and you go all out with a feast!'

His father said, 'Son, you don't understand. You're with me all the time, and everything that is mine is yours – but this is a wonderful time, and we had to celebrate. This brother of yours was dead, and he's alive! He was lost, and he's found!'

This story can be found in the Bible, in Luke's Gospel chapter 15, verses 11–32.

CHAPTER 1

PATIENT

Jesus told them this story: 'A man had two sons. The younger son told his father, "I want my share of your estate now, instead of waiting until you die." So his father agreed to divide his wealth between his sons' (Luke's Gospel 15:11–12).

Jesus of Nazareth is arguably the greatest teacher that has ever lived. No one else has succeeded in leaving their mark like Jesus has. It has been said that Socrates and Aristotle each taught for forty years, Plato for fifty years, but Jesus for only three. Yet his influence far surpasses the combined 130 years of teaching by these men who are acknowledged as the greatest philosophers of all antiquity. He painted no pictures, yet the finest paintings of Raphael, Michelangelo and Leonardo da Vinci received their illumination from him. He wrote no poetry, yet Dante, Milton and others of the world's greatest poets were inspired by him. He composed no music, yet Haydn, Handel, Beethoven and Bach achieved their highest perfection in hymns, symphonies and oratorios composed in his honour.

One of the main reasons why Jesus was such an extraordinary teacher was that he chose to use stories or parables as the primary vehicle for communicating eternal truths. In fact, in the Gospel of Mark we learn that Jesus used many stories and illustrations to teach the people, and that in his public teaching he only used parables (Mark 4:33–34). Many of these stories are still well known. In fact, they are so well known that their titles influence the way we speak about others: 'Oh, he's a Good Samaritan,' or, 'She's a prodigal.'

The story of the return of the prodigal son has been justly called 'the parable of parables'. Of all Jesus' stories, this one is commonly accepted as the pinnacle of his storytelling. It has affected and transformed lives throughout history.

BEGINNING AT THE BEGINNING

The parable of the prodigal son tells the tale of a young man who decides that he wants his inheritance before his father is dead. It's hard for many of us today to realise how utterly offensive this demand actually was. Those who have studied inheritance laws in the Middle East tell us that the request of the son was scandalous. To ask for your share of an estate before your father had died was, in Jesus' culture, totally dishonouring. It was tantamount to saying, 'I can't wait until you're dead. I want my inheritance now.' Furthermore, to sell your share of the estate while your father was still alive was to act with a total lack of decency. It was acting as if the father were already dead.

So the son's demand, 'I want my share of your estate now,' was the same as saying, 'Drop dead, Dad.' Selling this portion of the father's estate (implied in the story) was the same as saying to his father, 'You don't exist any more.'

Why did the younger son behave in this way? The parable gives us no answers to this question. I have always regarded it as interesting and potentially significant that a mother is not mentioned in this story. Certainly a Jewish mother is a very strong influence in a household and would have been expected to intervene. Could it be that the mother has died and that the son's behaviour is in part motivated by anger born from grief? It is impossible to say, and certainly we should not read too much into this. What we do know is that the boy made the demand. What we don't know is why.

What we also know is how the father responded to the demand. He did not beat the boy or berate him. He did not postpone the request or deny it. In fact he said yes and gave the sons their inheritance. This meant two-thirds of the estate for the older brother and one-third for the younger one. The reason for this inequality lies again in Jewish inheritance laws and in the right of the older son to the 'double blessing' due to the first-born. The father granted the demand and both boys received their share of the estate.

PATIENCE IS A VIRTUE

There is a lot we could say about the younger son at this point. Indeed, we could also make some comments about the older son who, according to cultural expectations, should have stood up for his father and told his younger brother not to be so impudent. But he does not step in to defend his father. And it is his father alone who comes out of this incident with credit. The two boys certainly don't. The father alone acts with integrity and dignity. It's *him* we should focus on.

What we have in the response of the dad in the opening to this story is a picture of great patience. Patience has been defined as a state of suffering with fortitude, as the ability to endure evils without complaining – evils such as toil, pain, poverty, insult, oppression, calamity and rejection. The word comes from the Latin *patiens*, meaning 'suffering', and has the idea of being able to endure much, to be 'long-suffering'. To be a patient person means to be a person who is able to endure severe blows and knocks without giving way to fury or to flight.

Needless to say, patience is not a quality or power that human beings find terribly easy. As the traditional rhyme goes,

Patience is a virtue,
Possess it if you can.
Found seldom in a woman,
Never in a man.

Patience is indeed a rare commodity, but those who have learned its secrets have discovered it to be an indispensable resource, especially in hard times. As Leonardo da Vinci once said, 'Patience serves as a protection against wrongs, as clothes do against cold. For if you put on more clothes as the cold increases, it will have no power to hurt you. So in like manner you must grow in patience when you meet with great wrongs, and they will then be powerless to vex your mind.'

THE HURTING FATHER

Let's be quite clear about what it was that the father suffered at the hands of his boy in the parable.

The one word that sums up the whole experience is the word 'rejection'.

The father first of all experienced the rejection of his person. When the prodigal son told his father that he wanted his inheritance right now, he was rejecting him. He was saying, 'I don't care whether you live or die. I reject *you*.' This was outrageous then and it is outrageous now. The boy was really saying, 'I don't want you. I want your money.' It's hard to imagine anything more hurtful.

Secondly, the father experienced the rejection of his history. The inheritance that the son was asking for was basically the sale of family land – land that would have been handed down to the father. In an agricultural society like this, land was handed down from one generation to another. The boy asked for this land to be converted into cash so that he could have a good time. That was the same as saying, 'I reject everything you have inherited from your father and your forefathers. I reject this family and don't wish to be associated with it any longer.'

Thirdly, the father experienced the rejection of his lifestyle. The boy was not asking for his share of the inheritance in order to set up another farm in another area. Nor was he seeking to establish some kind of relief for the poor. He wanted the money so that he could squander it in wild living. In doing this he was saying to his father, 'I reject everything you stand for.' Again, that was incredibly hurtful.

And yet, in spite of all this rejection, the father does not respond in kind. He does not lash out and reject his boy. Rather, he simply lets go. He doesn't say, 'OK, have your share. But I never want to see your face again.' Rather, he says in effect, 'OK. You may have what you have asked for. And you will have to experience the consequences of your poor choices. But I will never stop loving you. And I will always be here for you. Always.'

That's one very patient father.

OPEN HANDS, NOT CLENCHED FISTS

So the characteristic that is really remarkable about the father at the start of this story is his patience. He is dealt a terrific blow of injustice by his younger son's demand and an equally cruel blow of rejection by his older son's silence. Yet he does not explode with anger but rather with calm. He does not act to control his estate but rather he shows an amazing ability to release and let go. He does not attempt to stop his son but rather allows him to leave and go his own way. The more I think about this, as a father myself, the more I marvel at the father's character. He truly is a patient man.

Many parents today will tell you that they wish they had more of the virtue of patience. I love the story of the man in a supermarket who was pushing a trolley which contained, among other things, a screaming baby. As the man proceeded along the aisles, he kept repeating softly, 'Keep calm, George. Don't get excited, George. Don't get excited, George. Don't yell, George.'

A lady watching with admiration said to the man, 'You are certainly to be commended for your patience in trying to quiet little George.'

'Lady,' he declared, 'I'm George.'

That's a great picture of patience!

The father in Jesus' story was patient. He was on the receiving end of the most hurtful behaviour by both of his sons. Yet he responded patiently and calmly. He did not hold on to possessions or to people with clenched fists but rather held them lightly in his open, outstretched hands. Consequently, when the critical moment came, he was able to let go with his hands, even though he experienced indescribable agony in his heart.

The father experiences rejection but decides on a course of relinquishment. That takes great patience!

So What?

We need to remember that the story Jesus told was a parable. That means a down-to-earth story with a spiritual meaning. In other words, there are two levels to this 'parable of parables'. Level 1, the surface level, tells us the fictional events that occurred in the lives of a father and two sons. Level 2, the deeper level, tells us something that's spiritually significant. It tells us something about God and the way we as human beings relate to him, and he relates to us.

The main reason why I have written this book is because I am convinced that Jesus came to reveal what God is really like. The premier word he used in that respect was the word 'Father'. That is why in what is called 'the Lord's Prayer' he asks us to pray the words, 'Our Father in Heaven'. That is why you see Jesus everywhere calling God 'Father' and teaching about '*the* Father'. The truth is that Jesus came as the unique Son of God to disclose what the Father is like and to show us the way to go home. In his life, he provided a window onto the Father heart of God, proclaiming that 'anyone who has seen me has seen the Father' (John 14:9). In his teaching he made it clear that he alone revealed the

Father. As he says in Matthew's Gospel chapter 11, verse 27, 'My Father has given me authority over everything. No one really knows the Son except the Father, and no one really knows the Father except the Son and those to whom the Son chooses to reveal him.'

When Jesus chose to speak about God, the word he used was 'Father'. He chose, in other words, 'paternal' imagery when he taught about God. At times God is also described in maternal ways as well – as having qualities that we associate with being a good mother. In using paternal and occasionally maternal language about God, the Bible is basically saying that God is a divine parent and that he knows something about parenting. Indeed, he invented it! When Jesus talks about the father in the parable, I believe he is pointing to his Father in heaven. He is saying, 'This parent is your divine parent.'

THE LONG-SUFFERING FATHER

It is a sad fact that human beings so often make poor choices when it comes to God. In fact, throughout recent decades in the west, we have effectively behaved towards God in the way the younger son behaved in the parable. We have really told God to 'drop dead' and we have behaved as if he did not exist. This has meant abandoning the Ten Commandments in most societies and it has also meant an advocacy of secularism, atheism and even nihilism in many aspects of culture.

I remember seeing, when I was a student, something someone had written on the back of a toilet door. It said 'God is dead' and it was signed 'Nietzsche'. That was really the prevailing philosophy when I was a student. There was also, however, another message on the toilet door. Under 'God is dead', signed 'Nietzsche', someone had written, 'Nietzsche is dead', signed 'God'.

If I think about it, God has had to endure patiently a great deal of rebellion and rejection by human beings throughout the millennia. From our earliest human ancestors, men and women have been telling him that he's as good as dead and behaving as if he didn't exist. Today's world is no exception. There is still a widespread tendency to neglect or reject God. How does even a loving God put up with us? Why doesn't he simply strike the earth with a celestial laser and start all over again, with a better model of responsive humanity?

The Jewish people have a story that I think gives the answer.

According to the Hebrew tale, their great forefather Abraham was one day sitting outside his tent minding his own business when he saw an old man, weary from a long journey, walking slowly towards him. Being a very hospitable man, Abraham welcomed him, washed his feet, cooked some food and gave him an evening meal. As the man started eating, Abraham noticed he didn't give thanks to God before he started eating, so he challenged him, saying, 'Are you not a worshipper of God?'

The old man replied, 'The only god I worship is fire. I don't honour any other god.'

Hearing this, Abraham became very angry, took hold of the man aggressively and threw him out of his tent into the cold night. When the old man had left the vicinity, God paid Abraham a visit and asked him to explain his actions. Abraham said to God, 'I kicked the old man out because he refused to acknowledge and honour you.'

To which God replied, 'I have patiently endured this man for over eighty years. Could you not endure him for just one night?'

The reason why God does not wipe out his creation is simply that he is a long-suffering Father. Like the dad in the parable, God has had to put up with being rejected. As C.S. Lewis once wrote of the first human beings:

As a young man wants a regular allowance from his father which he can count on as his own . . . so they desired to be on their own, to take care for their own future, to plan for pleasure and security. . . . They wanted, as we say, to 'call their souls their own'. But that means to live a lie, for our souls are not, in fact, our own. They wanted some corner of the universe of which they could say to God, 'This is our business, not yours.' But there is no such corner.

The truth is that our Heavenly Father is patient. The Bible says that he is 'slow to anger and rich in love' (Psalm 145:8, New International Version (NIV)). The Bible also makes the point that God has been patient with people throughout history. The prophet Nehemiah says about God's people, 'You were patient with them for many years' (Nehemiah 9:30). Saint Peter also says that the Lord 'is being patient for your sake. He does not want anyone to perish' (2 Peter 3:9). Saint Paul says, 'love is patient' (1 Corinthians 13:4) and Saint John says 'God is love' (1 John 4:16). God is a loving, patient Father who shows the kind of patience the father of the prodigal son exhibits in Luke chapter 15.

THE MOST PATIENT PARENT

We have a patient Father in heaven. That's the first thing we learn from this story. You may have actively rejected him, as the younger son did his father, or you may have simply neglected him. You may have said, 'Drop dead,' or simply behaved as if he didn't exist. Either way, he is enduring the agony of our rebellion with incredible patience.

Saint Paul challenged his readers in the first century by appealing to the Father's patient love. Writing in the second chapter of his letter to the Romans, he said in verse 4, 'Don't you realize how kind, tolerant, and patient God is with you? Or don't you care? Can't you see how kind he has been in giving you time to turn from your sin?' Here the word translated 'patient' means two things: the attitude of one who never gives up and eventually reaps the reward, and that of one who could retaliate and take revenge but chooses not to.

Later, Saint Paul wrote about how God was patient with him personally. For a long time Saint Paul was known as Saul. He persecuted those who believed in Jesus Christ in the very early days of the church. Then, as Saul was on his way to Damascus to cause the church even more suffering, Jesus Christ appeared to him in a vision. Saul was utterly transformed. He would say he was 'saved'. He became Paul and started promoting the very faith he had persecuted. And Saint Paul attributed all this to the patience of God. In his first letter to Timothy (chapter 1, verses 15–16) he wrote,

This is a true saying, and everyone should believe it: Christ Jesus came into the world to save sinners – and I was the worst of them all. But that is why God had mercy on me, so that Christ Jesus could use me as a prime example of his great patience with even the worst sinners.

To put it another way, Saint Paul was saying, 'God was incredibly patient with me!'

In all of this, the message is that we have a very patient heavenly Father who, like the dad in the parable, is giving us time to turn round, come home and experience his embrace. 'Patience,' said John Ciardi, 'is the art of caring very slowly.'

More than that, patience is absolutely fundamental to all our relationships. As Lawrence Lovasik has written, 'The practice of patience toward one another . . . is the most elementary condition of all human and social activity.' As you read on, my prayer is that you will not presume on that divine patience any longer than you need to, but that you will see what the Father is truly like, and come running home.

CHAPTER 2

WAITING

So he returned home to his father. And while he was still a long distance away, his father saw him coming (Luke's Gospel 15:20).

My all-time favourite Christmas film is *It's a Wonderful Life* (1946). Directed by Frank Capra and starring James Stewart, *It's a Wonderful Life* tells the story of a man called George Bailey who lives in a town called Bedford Falls. George Bailey is a dreamer. He dreams of going to college, travelling the world and becoming an architect. But his dad dies and George is told that the only way his father's business can survive is if he takes it over. Forgoing all his own plans, George takes on the business, gets married and settles down to a humdrum life in Bedford Falls.

One day, disaster strikes. George's Uncle Billy loses a large sum of money belonging to the business and cannot find it. At this point, George cracks. After an hour of watching him function as a happy-go-lucky Everyman, we now see him disintegrate before our very eyes. He berates his affable uncle for losing the money. He shouts at his wife and children. He loses his temper with the teacher of one of his children over the telephone, and he pours scorn upon the faults in his house. It seems as if it's a wonderful life for everyone except George Bailey.

In desperation George runs out of his house and heads for the local bar. He drinks too much as he sits in a state of mental agony. At his lowest point, he puts his head in his hands and pours his heart out in the form of a prayer – one of cinema's greatest ever prayers. He confesses he is not a praying man and then says, 'Dear Father, if you're up there and you can hear me, please show me the way. I'm at the end of my rope. Show me the way.'

That is the turning point in the movie. God indeed answers his prayer, but not in the way George Bailey expected. To see just how, you need to watch the film yourself!

RETURNING TO THE FATHER

At his moment of greatest despair, George Bailey remembered the God of his childhood, the one whom Jesus taught us to call Father. This marked the beginning of his homecoming, of his healing and restoration.

What was true for George Bailey was true also for the younger son in the 'parable of parables'. We left the story at the point when the boy stormed out of his house with the money from his share of the estate, leaving his father devastated at home.

Jesus tells us that the boy travelled to a distant land and wasted his father's hard-earned money on 'wild living'. Later on, from what his older brother says, we can infer that part of the inheritance was spent on having sex with prostitutes.

What we are talking about here is an addictive lifestyle. Addiction is a process in which a person becomes dependent on a mood-altering substance or behaviour, leading to greater and greater excess and to a loss of control. Those who are experts in the field point to the roots of such behaviour patterns, not just the symptoms. At the core of almost every addicted person is a hole in the soul. The addicted person is basically looking for love in all the wrong places.

The younger son, overly attached to money and sex, eventually loses everything. When his money runs out, a great famine sweeps over the land and he begins to starve. Desperate for cash, he persuades a local farmer to hire him to feed the pigs. For a Jewish boy this was nothing short of absolute humiliation. 'Cursed are those who breed swine,' said the rabbis. But the boy will stop at nothing. He becomes so hungry that even the carob pods the pigs are eating look appetising.

But the boy is not just hungry for food; he is also hungry for his father's love. So, at his lowest point ('hitting bottom', to use the technical phrase), he comes to his senses and does what George Bailey does. He starts to think about his father, saying the following words to himself:

> *I will go home to my father and say, 'Father, I have sinned against both heaven and you, and I am no longer worthy of being called your son. Please take me on as a hired man'* (Luke 15:18–19).

With this resolution in his heart, the younger son begins his journey home.

WHAT WAS DAD DOING BACK HOME?

One of the critical questions for us to ask at this point is this: what was the father doing while his son was away? The answer is obvious from the parable. The father was waiting every day for his son to return. Day and night, it seems, the father was waiting at the gates of his house, or his village, looking attentively in the direction his son had gone, desperately longing for a reunion with his lost boy.

This is some father!

As Jesus records, while the boy was still a long way off, the father saw him coming home.

Lovesick for his son, the father had been watching and waiting for a long time – long enough for his son to squander a fortune, get a job in a pig farm, and ride out part of a famine. Who knows how many days he squinted in the sunlight, peering into the distant horizon, scanning the landscape for the silhouette of a man, for the slightest hint of movement? Who knows how many nights he lit a torch and walked the boundaries of his home, watched by his bemused neighbours as he held the flame aloft and waved it from side to side, shouting his son's name? Who knows how much humiliation the father endured from those who saw him behave like this?

It's possible, of course, that the father shared this responsibility of waiting, though Jesus never says this in the story. If the mother were still alive, it's possible that she might have been waiting. Although she is never mentioned in the story, someone has imagined how she would have felt, as a mother, in this situation. They have expressed this in the form of a poem, entitled 'The mother of the prodigal son':

Where is the mother of the prodigal son
On that day so long ago?
What were her thoughts
And what were her fears
As she watched him turn to go?

How many times in the dark of night
Did the tears slide down her face?
Did she get out of bed
And fall on her knees,
Just to pray that her boy was safe?

How were the days when she did not know . . .
Was he alive? Was he warm? Was he well?
Who were his friends?
And where did he sleep?
Was there anyone there she could tell?

But, oh, on that day when she looked down the road
As she had looked since her son went away,
Did love unspeakable flood her soul?
Did she cry?
What did she say?

I think when the father had welcomed their son
And the boy had greeted his brother,
That the servants made a path
For him to enter the door
And the waiting arms of his mother.

We don't know if the mother was still alive, but if she was,
she would have been waiting – attentively watching for her
absent son. As the poem above suggests, that waiting would
have been characterized by an aching heart. What we do
know is that the father was still alive, and that he was
watching. The simple word 'saw' in the statement 'the father
saw him coming' suggests that.

In a sense, the son had lost everything. He had lost his
home. He had lost his money. He had lost his dignity. He had

lost his reputation. He had lost his security. He had lost his honour. But the one thing he never lost was his father's love. The father waited.

THE AGONY OF WAITING

It is a hard thing for a parent whose child runs away from home. It is a tough thing for a parent whose child stays at home and yet runs away from love. In both cases, the parent is left worrying over the choices the child is making, longing for a change of heart. Those who have to endure such times of waiting know this.

I remember when one of my children decided in his early teens that he wanted nothing more to do with God. Ordinarily that might not be such a problem for some parents, but I happen to be a vicar, and my faith is more precious to me than anything. So when my child chose to rebel against God and to reject all that we held dear it was a difficult time.

For over a year I wanted so much to be able to connect with my son. He was present in my house but he was absent emotionally and spiritually. What could my wife and I do?

I remember right at the start of this time praying earnestly to God and asking for help. In my place of desperation he heard my cry and reminded me of the parable of the prodigal son. He pointed to the waiting father in the story, who had completely let go of his son, and I sensed him saying, 'I want you to be like that. Just watch and pray.

Don't preach at him. Be quiet and accepting, like the father in the story.'

So that is what I did. I watched and prayed. Through those long months of a very public rebellion, I just waited with a lovesick heart for my son to come back.

One Monday morning, over a year later, I was preparing to leave home to travel to Norway. As I poured myself a cup of coffee, my son came into the kitchen and whispered in my ear that he had something he wanted me to know before I left. He then told me that he had been about to go to sleep the night before when he sensed the presence of God in his bedroom, and a voice saying, 'I love you, child.' He knew that it was his Heavenly Father and there and then he said sorry to God and gave his heart to the Lord. And then he threw his arms around me.

I cannot begin to put into words what I felt after all those months of waiting. It is hard to write about it even now. But one thing I do know is that I had to let go out of sheer obedience and give my son back to the perfect Father. And when I relinquished control like that, God himself came to my son's rescue and saved him from things that I dare not speak about.

SO WHAT?

The Bible as a whole tells the Father's story. In the early parts of the Bible we see God adopting one small nation from all the nations of the world. This nation was called Israel and the Father adopted this people not because there was anything inherently special about them but because he wanted to make them the agents of his love and blessing to the world. Having been adopted, the people of Israel chose to rebel against their Father. As a result of their disobedience, God's people lost their home in Jerusalem and left Judah for exile in a foreign land (Babylon, modern Iraq). Like the prodigal son, God's people left home and lived with the consequences of their rebellion against the Father. All this happened six hundred years before Jesus of Nazareth was born.

While God's people were far away from their homeland, the Father waited with a broken heart for them to turn back to him and come home into his arms of love. The Old Testament prophet Jeremiah sees right into the Father heart of God during the time of the exile and gives voice to the aching wound he finds there:

'Is not Israel still my son, my darling child?' asks the LORD.
'I had to punish him, but I still love him. I long for him and
surely will have mercy on him' (Jeremiah 31:20).

This great cry from the heart of God shows how God saw himself as Israel's Father and Israel as his 'son', his 'darling child'. There is no mistaking the intensity of the affection in these words.

Although Israel had chosen to reject the Father, leading to the punishment of having to live far away from home, the Father calls to his child to return. In the words you are about to read, the Father changes his way of speaking about Israel. Instead of calling Israel his son, he refers to the nation as 'my virgin Israel', 'my wayward daughter':

> Set up road signs; put up guideposts. Mark well the path by which you came. Come back again, my virgin Israel; return to your cities here. How long will you wander, my wayward daughter? For the LORD will cause something new and different to happen – Israel will embrace her God (Jeremiah 31:21–22).

What great words these are! In every sentence of this passage from the prophet Jeremiah we catch a glimpse of 'the waiting Father'. The Father pours out his heart to Israel through his servant the prophet. He talks of 'longing' for his boy and he appeals to his daughter to stop wandering and to 'come back again'. His heart yearns for Israel, his beloved daughter, to experience the Father's 'embrace' again. What an amazing picture of the Father heart of God.

WHEN THE TIME WAS FULLY COME

Well, the Jewish people did return from Babylon to Jerusalem and rebuilt both the Temple and the city, in the sixth and fifth centuries BC. But far more was needed than just the rebuilding of the Father's house and the restoration of the city of God. For Jeremiah's prophecy to be fulfilled, for the embrace of God to be experienced, something much greater was required than just a rebuilding project. The Jewish people needed to have the God of the Temple, not just the Temple of God. They needed God to come to his Temple and to open up a new way of knowing and loving him. They needed, in short, a visitation from heaven.

And so God the Father waited a little longer. Four centuries in fact. He waited until everything was in place and then he sent his one and only Son, Jesus. As Saint Paul puts it in his letter to the Galatians,

> *But when the right time came, God sent his Son, born of a woman, subject to the law. God sent him to buy freedom for us who were slaves to the law, so that he could adopt us as his very own children (Galatians 4:4–5).*

We need to note those words, 'when the right time came'. The Father waited until absolutely the right moment before sending his only Son to reconcile us to himself and adopt us into his family. Jesus was born at a precise moment in space and time – a time ordained by God in heaven, and a place pinpointed by the Father, Bethlehem. The birth of Jesus was a well planned event that occurred when the conditions were right. At the perfect point in human history, God himself entered our world in the person of his beloved Son.

Why was the time so right?

First, the timing was perfect politically. At the time of Jesus' birth, Israel was under Roman occupation. The enforcement of Roman law in the land of Israel ironically helped the Father to fulfil his purposes. When the Roman Emperor, Augustus, called for a census throughout the Empire, Joseph and Mary had to travel from their home town of Nazareth to Bethlehem to record their details. This meant that the Old Testament prophecy concerning the birthplace of the Messiah would be fulfilled. The prophet Micah had foreseen the importance of Bethlehem in God's great plan. Now that prophecy was fulfilled.

Second, the timing was perfect historically. The Roman Empire enjoyed a generation of great peace before Jesus' birth. This enabled the government to concentrate on building, rather than going to war. Thanks to the Roman army throughout the Empire, the most amazing system of roads and bridges had been built, enabling people to travel in ways they could never have done before. This meant that the message of Jesus would spread very quickly.

Third, the timing was perfect culturally. Thanks to the conquests of Alexander the Great 350 years before Jesus' birth, the main language throughout the Roman Empire was, in fact, a popular kind of Greek. Having one such language would again help the message of Jesus to spread much faster. When the Gospels came to be written, they were written in this same market place Greek, and this meant that they could be quickly understood by the widest possible number of people.

Fourth, the timing was perfect philosophically. People were actually expecting God to do something amazing at this time, and not just the Jewish people either. Even one of Rome's greatest poets, Virgil, wrote a poem about the birth of a divine child who would bring peace to the world (the poem is called 'Virgil's Fourth Eclogue'). The philosophers and poets of the age were expectant. Even some of the astronomers were too, as the story of the wise men reveals.

Finally, the timing was perfect religiously. Once the Temple was rebuilt, the sacrifices could begin again, including the annual sacrifice of the Passover Lamb. This would provide an extremely significant backdrop for Jesus' ministry. As the prophet John the Baptist declared, when he first saw Jesus, 'Behold, the Lamb of God who takes away the sin of the world.'

THE WAITING FATHER

When Saint Paul said that Jesus was born 'when the time was right', he meant something very special by the word 'time'. The word he uses means not ordinary chronological time but a special moment that will never be repeated. In the

1970s rock opera *Jesus Christ Superstar*, Judas Iscariot asks Jesus, 'Why did you choose to come right now?' The truth is that the Father had been waiting patiently for all the right conditions to prevail. He had been waiting, and he had been waiting actively, not passively. This waiting was not a cold, detached activity. It was a full-on, heartfelt waiting based on an intense longing for restored intimacy. To put it simply, the Father waited in history as the father waited in the parable.

But what meaning does the word 'wait' really have in relation to God?

A few years before my adoptive father died, he asked to see me. I went into his study and we sat together. He was not well at all and his thoughts were much concerned with dying and death. I remember so vividly the questions he asked me.

'Son, is there time as we know it in heaven?'

I remember replying that I doubted it. It seemed to me then and it seems to me now that heaven is a dimension beyond space and time. Therefore, the temporal coordinates with which we are concerned don't concern those in the heavenly realms.

This provoked a second question.

'If there is no time in heaven, there must be no consciousness of time passing, and that means there can be no sense of waiting for something future to come to pass.'

I remember replying that this seemed logical, though heaven's mysteries may not be unlocked by the key of logic alone.

Then Dad asked me his final question.

'If there is no time in heaven, and there is no consciousness of waiting, won't that mean that when I die I won't have to wait for you in heaven, even though you are still living here on earth?'

That was some question!

I don't know what currency the word 'wait' has for God. What I do know is that Jesus was trying to say something incredibly significant about his Father when he told the parable of parables. He was trying to tell us that our Father in heaven waits for us to return to his arms of love, and that this waiting involves watching with tear-filled eyes. Most dads have to wait for their children. God is also, and supremely, the waiting Father. And he's waiting for you too.

CHAPTER 3

COMPASSIONATE

Filled with love and compassion . . . (Luke's Gospel 15:20).

Michele Campbell tells a very moving story called 'Daddy's Little Girl'. The story begins with the words, 'Will you tell Daddy for me?' A 17-year-old girl is pregnant and she is asking her mother to tell her father. Having had a very close relationship with her dad, and having always been 'daddy's little girl', she knows that he will be shattered. Her mother agrees and drops the daughter off at a Christian minister's house as she tells her husband the news.

Meanwhile, the daughter waits at the minister's house, being consoled and counselled. The minister, not judging her, prays with her as they wait. Then, all of a sudden, the daughter sees the headlights of a car arriving. The daughter, called Missy, runs into the bathroom and locks the door. But the minister gently reprimands her and she comes out, trembling. She is not afraid of her father's anger. She is terrified that she will no longer be her father's 'little girl'.

She hears the footsteps on the sidewalk and the light tap on the door. Her lip quivers, followed by a flood of tears. She hides behind the minister's tall frame. Her mother comes in first, smiling, her eyes swollen with tears. And then he is there.

Missy's father doesn't even stop to say a word to the minister. He strides straight past him and comes to his daughter and gathers her up in his arms. He holds her close and whispers, 'I love you, I love you, and I will love your baby too.'

Missy barely manages to say it, but she replies, 'I'm sorry, Daddy. I love you so much.'

'I know. Let's go home.'

And home they go, all fear gone. Missy knows there are hard times ahead, but she also knows that she is still Daddy's little girl. Recognising that, there isn't a storm she can't weather.

THE COMPASSIONATE FATHER

Michele Campbell's story gives a great picture of a compassionate father.

And so does the parable that Jesus told.

This father's child had rebelled and gone off the rails, big time. But every day the father had been looking. Whenever a merchant came into the village, the father would probably have asked, 'Have you seen him? Have you seen my son? A young lad with dark hair, dark eyes. Wealthy too. His name is Jacob. Have you seen him on your travels, especially in the far country?'

And yet again he would see that blank stare, that look that signalled 'no'.

Every day the father had lived with the gossip and the rumour-mongering in the village. He had grown used to walking through groups of villagers who would suddenly stop speaking as he drew near, only to start their conversation again in hushed and hurried tones as soon as he had walked past. He knew they were talking about his son. He knew they were discussing the shame and dishonour of his son's name.

Every night the father had stayed awake and no one ever saw the tears that streamed down his face as he relived the agonising day of his son's departure. No one saw the heaving of his shoulders as he gave way to quiet grief. And no one ever heard the cry of his heart through the watches of the night, 'Oh my son, my beloved son, my son . . . please come home.'

And yet the pilot light of his love for his boy never went out. Every day it continued to burn until one evening, sitting on the flat roof of his house, he saw something. Engaged for a thousand times in what the villagers had called the hopeless vigil of a silly old man, he had suddenly caught a glimpse of a familiar outline. He rubbed his eyes, blinked, and peered again. Could it be?

And then the beating of his heart, the hands over his head in shock, the hesitation, and finally the certainty. 'It's my boy,' he shouted. 'My son is coming home. Oh, my son. My son . . .'

WHAT IS COMPASSION?

What we're talking about here is compassion. Compassion means literally to suffer with someone in their pain and distress. It means to come alongside someone in their suffering and to feel what they feel. It means far more than just pity – it means empathic love. It means the engagement of both the heart and the hand – the heart in sharing in another's pain, the hand in reaching out to help. Compassion, in short, is about participation, not detachment. It is about actions more than words. It is about equality, not superiority. It is about 'suffering love'.

When Jesus says in the parable that the father was filled with 'compassion', the word he uses is significant. In the original manuscripts of the New Testament, the language used is Greek. The Greek word for 'compassion' has the word for 'guts' or 'bowels' contained within it. When the father is said to be filled with 'compassion' towards his son, the emotion that he felt was not superficial but profound. It went even deeper than the heart, to the guts. It was visceral pity.

Part of the reason for this way of speaking lies in the ancient Middle Eastern view that a person's emotions were based in their abdomen. When a Middle Eastern person felt compassion, they felt it in their 'innards'. Even today, when hearing a pitiful tale, Middle Eastern people will commonly say, 'You are cutting up my intestines' rather than 'breaking my heart'.

Going back to the parable, it is really important for us to understand that the father felt this kind of gut-wrenching emotion towards his son. This was not deep-seated anger coming to the surface. It was the deep-seated sense of pity and concern that made the dad sick to his stomach. Seeing his son walking down the road looking so beaten up by life, the father couldn't help himself. His emotions welled up from the pit of his stomach and, as we will see in the next chapter, this emotion resulted in motion. No sooner had he felt this pain than he was racing towards his son, desperate to hug and to hold him, to reassure him that he was still 'Daddy's child'.

SUFFERING LOVE IN ACTION

This picture of the father literally racing towards his son reminds me of a true story about a dad who ran to his son in an athletics event.

Recently I watched a programme on television called *The 100 Greatest Sporting Moments*. The incident that most inspired me was not the one that came first. In fact, it did not even feature in the top fifty. But for me it was the best of the best.

During the Barcelona Olympics in 1992, British athlete Derek Redmon ran in the 400 metres semi-finals. This was the fulfilment of a dream. But 100 metres into the race he fell on the track, having torn a hamstring. The other athletes ran past him and all of them finished the race. Redmon's dreams of running in a final were shattered. He got to his feet and started to limp towards the finish but he was in terrible agony and could barely move.

At that moment, a man leaped over the security fence separating the track from the spectators. He ran towards the hobbling athlete as security guards tried to stop him. He even pushed one of the guards over.

Derek Redmon waved the guards away as the man – a big guy, older than Derek, and wearing a Nike cap that said 'Just do it!' – lifted Derek's arm over his shoulder and started to walk with him slowly towards the finishing line, supporting him all the way.

As the older man kept speaking words of encouragement to Redmon, the crowd began to switch their attention from the athletes who had finished to this strange sight of two men struggling to the finish. As they began to appreciate what was happening, they started to roar their approval. It was said that when Derek Redmon crossed the finishing line the ovation was greater than for any other achievement in the Games. The crowd was not to know until later that the man who helped this stricken athlete was none other than

Derek Redmon's dad, Jim. His father, seeing his son's distress, came alongside him and helped him finish the race.

Now that, to me, is the greatest ever sporting moment! Someone has said that 'triumph' is a combination of 'try' and 'oomph'! If that's true, then Derek Redmon's finish was truly a triumph. He didn't win a medal, but he did win the hearts of every spectator who was there at the time, and everyone who has watched the incident since.

Derek Redmon's dad was truly a father of compassion – a father who demonstrated suffering love in action. Like the father of the son in the parable, this father was filled with love. He was moved deeply and he acted on his feelings in a way that was 100 per cent self-forgetful. Both the father of the prodigal son and the father of the fallen athlete display 'compassion'.

SO WHAT?

Once again, in the simple words 'filled with compassion', Jesus was not just describing the father of the prodigal son; he was also telling us something about his Father in heaven. In the Book of Psalms we read this about God in Psalm 103, verse 13 (NIV):

As a father has compassion on his children, so the LORD has compassion on those who fear him.

What King David (who wrote this psalm) is saying is this: that the God of the Bible is not a detached and absent God. He is not the apathetic God of the ancient Greeks, incapable of experiencing suffering. Rather, he is a Father who feels what we feel and feels it acutely.

This is really important. Too many people today operate with an ancient Greek view of what God is like. They see God as aloof from our pain. But the Bible reveals quite a different picture of God. Indeed, in the shortest verse of the Bible we read, 'Jesus wept' (John 11:35). This was at the funeral of a friend called Lazarus. John reports that Jesus sobbed when he came to Lazarus' tomb.

Not long ago I was asked to speak at a conference for women who had been adopted, who had given up a child for adoption or who had themselves adopted a child. I was asked to address the spiritual issues to do with being orphaned. I spoke about my experiences of being abandoned and adopted, and used these to describe my journey into new life as an adopted son of my Heavenly Father. Afterwards, the conference organizer wrote about what God had done among the women at that conference. She told the following story:

I had the privilege of praying for a young woman whose father had died when she was five. She had walked into the kitchen to find him dead on the floor from a heart attack. She was quickly hustled out and then it was presumed that she was too young to grieve. All the pain was locked in her heart and she has lived for years in a grey world, finding it difficult to relate to God as Father.

When we prayed, I spoke about Lazarus and how Jesus wept and how that was an expression of the Father's tender heart. I felt that when Jesus saw her father and how she would be brought up without a dad, he wept for her. She started weeping and through tears explained that her maiden name was Lazarus and that literally Lazarus had died! She felt she was in the very centre of the Father's focus and love, and that he wanted her to know that. That is just my story, but there were many others like this where God was doing a deep healing work.

The Bible says that Jesus alone reveals the Father. Jesus himself said that anyone who had seen him had seen the Father. In other words, he was the truest reflection of what our Heavenly Father is really like. If that is really true – and you and I need to decide whether it is – then the two words 'Jesus wept' are filled with extraordinary meaning. They tell us that God weeps when we suffer, that he is not remote and aloof from our pain, but that he truly understands. Jesus reveals that our Father in heaven is like the dad in the parable of parables. He is filled with compassion. He agonises over our tragedies with suffering love.

THE GOD WHO IS WITH US

Nothing highlights this more than the extraordinary truth celebrated every Christmas Day, the birth of Jesus of Nazareth. For Christians, the birth of Jesus marks the moment when the infinite becomes an infant. It signals the entrance of the Living God into history, in the form of a baby. Now nothing could be more mysterious than this – the Great God of the Universe appearing in human flesh as a tiny, helpless child. But this is exactly what is unique about Christianity. Christianity is not like other religions. It does not present us with rules and rituals designed to help human beings climb up to where God is. Rather, it shows how God stepped down from heaven to earth to re-establish intimacy with us. As theologians have often put it, God participated in our human nature so we could participate in his divine nature.

In doing this, the God of the Bible became Immanuel, a name given to Jesus that means 'God with us'. With the arrival of Jesus, God is no longer God against us, or above us, but among us. Born as a baby in a feeding trough behind a Bethlehem pub, Jesus spent his first few years on the run with his parents, trying to escape a murderous tyrant called Herod. He then returned to Nazareth where he grew to be an adult, doing a mundane job in his father's carpentry shop and studying the Old Testament with the local rabbi. He began a three-year ministry when he was about 30, and he was criticised and insulted by the religious authorities along the way. Three years later he was tortured and then killed on a Roman cross, the most painful death imaginable. Three days later, his followers saw him alive again.

All the painful events that Jesus experienced show that God understands what it is to be human, what it is to suffer, and what it is to die a painful death. If Jesus is God's Son, and God's Son experienced all the agonies of the human condition, it means that human suffering is in the Godhead. If human suffering has been experienced by God himself, then we can be 100 per cent sure that our Father in heaven is the one who truly understands.

THE GOD OF THE SCARS

For me, the poet Edward Stillito expressed this thought most powerfully in the following words:

> The other gods were strong, but you were weak.
> They rode, but you did stumble to a throne;
> But to our wounds, only God's wounds can speak,
> And not a god has wounds, but you alone.

The point the poet is making is that Jesus is the only deity in the entire course of history, and indeed in the arena of world religions, who has suffered the worst angst and agony of a human life. Other gods are nearly always portrayed as conquering through strength. But Jesus Christ conquers through suffering love and the power of weakness. He is truly unique.

Consider the following:

More than two thousand years ago there was a man born contrary to the laws of life. He lived in poverty and was reared in obscurity. He did not travel extensively. Only once did he cross the boundary of the country in which he lived; that was during his exile in childhood as a refugee.

He possessed neither wealth nor influence. His relatives were inconspicuous, and had neither training nor formal education.

In infancy he startled a king; in childhood he puzzled doctors; in manhood he ruled the course of nature. He walked upon the waves as if pavements, and he hushed the sea to sleep.

He healed the multitudes without medicine and made no charge for his service.

He never wrote a book, and yet all the libraries of the country could not hold the books that have been written about him.

He never wrote a song, and yet he has furnished the

theme for more songs than all the songwriters combined.

He never founded a college, but all the schools put together cannot boast of having as many students.

He never marshalled an army, nor drafted a soldier, nor fired a gun; and yet no leader ever had more volunteers who have, under his orders, made more rebels stack arms and surrender without a shot fired.

He never practised psychiatry, and yet he has healed more broken hearts than all the doctors far and near.

Once each week the wheels of commerce cease their turning and multitudes wend their way to worshipping assemblies to pay homage and respect to him.

The names of the past proud statesman of Greece and Rome have come and gone. The names of the past scientists, philosophers and theologians have come and gone; but the name of this Man abounds more and more. Though time has spread more than two thousand years between people of this generation and the scene of his crucifixion, yet he still lives. Herod could not destroy him, and the grave could not hold him.

He began earthly life in a humble stable but now he stands forth upon the highest pinnacle of heavenly glory, proclaimed of God, acknowledged by angels, adored by saints and feared by devils, as the living Jesus Christ, Lord and Saviour.

Jesus of Nazareth truly is unique. There are many reasons for this but chief among them is his compassion. Jesus is often described in the Gospels as being 'moved with compassion'. He went to the cross and died for the world because of this compassion. The thing that pretty well everyone admires about Jesus, even the cynics, is his undeniable compassion. This King understands. He suffers with his people. He truly is God with us.

THE ONE WHO TRULY UNDERSTANDS

A lady called Jill Briscoe once had to speak at a church in Croatia where two hundred newly arrived refugees were gathered. Her audience was mostly women, because the men were either dead, imprisoned or at war. After seeing the women's faces, she felt that her message was totally inappropriate for them. So she prayed for God to give her the words to say.

Putting aside her notes, she started to tell the women about Jesus and how as a child he had become a refugee himself. She told of how his parents had had to flee to Egypt pursued by Herod's soldiers and how they had left everything behind. She told of the rest of Jesus' life too, and finished by describing what Jesus had suffered on the Cross. She told it as it was, not as in the pictures – Jesus, hanging naked on the Cross. She finished her message by saying, 'All these things have happened to you. You are homeless. You have had to flee. You have suffered unjustly. But you didn't have a choice. He had a choice. He knew all this would happen to him but he still came.' Then Jill told them why.

Many of the refugees knelt down, put their hands in the air and wept. 'He's the only one who really understands,' they cried.

This is the Father revealed by Jesus – a compassionate Father, a Father who suffers with his children.

It may be that you never had a dad who was there for you, who suffered with you, and who yearned for you like the father in the parable. Maybe he was absent physically. Maybe he was absent emotionally. When you suffered, he was not there to protect, to help, to advise and, above all, to show compassion. The good news is that you have a perfect Father in heaven. Jesus came to show us what God is truly like. The word he used to describe and address God was the Aramaic word *Abba*, meaning 'dear father'. Through his life, death and resurrection, Jesus has made it possible for us to know God as Daddy and to call him 'Father'.

If you feel far away from God, remember the Father Jesus revealed in the parable of parables. He is waiting for you to come home. His heart is not filled with anger and hatred towards you. Even though you may have rejected or just neglected him, he is slow to anger and abounding in love. So come on home. As you make that choice, know that your Father in heaven is filled with compassion for you, that he understands, that his heart is for you and his arms are opened wide.

CHAPTER 4

RUNNING

He ran to his son . . . (Luke's Gospel 15:20).

As a father myself, I am always inspired by stories about great fathers. One of the most inspiring examples of all is a man called Dick Hoyt, now in his sixties. Dick Hoyt has a son called Rick. Rick was born in 1962 with his umbilical cord coiled around his neck. The oxygen to Rick's brain was cut off and his parents were told there was no hope for their child's future development. When he was eight months old, Rick's mum and dad were told that their son, who had cerebral palsy, would be a vegetable all his life.

Today, Dick and Rick are two of the most famous athletes in America. As a father-and-son team, they compete in marathon races – Dad running and pulling his quadriplegic son on a cart behind him. In recent years they have been taking part in the gruelling Iron Man competitions – triathlon competitions involving running a marathon, swimming 2.4 miles and cycling 112 miles. Even though

Rick cannot walk or talk, he is carried, pulled and towed by his dad for miles and miles in arduous conditions and extraordinary feats.

Not long ago, Rick typed out his story. He began, 'Dad is one of my role models. Once he sets out to do something, Dad sticks to it, whatever it is, until it is done. . . . Dad, I cannot find the words to express my gratitude to you for pushing me. . . . Dad, when I'm running, it feels like I'm not even handicapped. . . . I love you, man.'

I have a DVD with five minutes of film in which this remarkable father and son perform the triathlon to the soundtrack, 'I Know That My Redeemer Lives'. When I show it to audiences, there is rarely a heart unmoved. It is an inspiring picture of fatherly dedication. And it is a great parable of the Father whom Jesus reveals – a Father who loves everyone deeply, who excludes nobody, and who carries us through the trials of life. As Rick says, 'There isn't anything we can't do together.'

In the last chapter I told the story of Derek Redmon's father, Jim. Jim Redmon ran to his son when Derek fell on the racetrack in the 400 metres semi-final at the Barcelona Olympics. Putting his son's arm around his shoulder, Jim helped him across the finishing line to the sound of thunderous applause.

This picture of the father running to his stricken son is a stirring and inspirational one, like the picture of Dick Hoyt running with his son in his arms. But in some ways neither of these great pictures is as stirring and inspiring as the one in the parable of parables. For the son in the Olympic race had done nothing wrong, had done nothing to offend his father. Nor had Rick Hoyt. On the other hand, the son in the parable had done dreadful things to his father, things that in his own Middle Eastern culture were indescribably shameful. Not only had he asked for his inheritance while his father was still alive, he had also squandered that hard-earned fortune on what Jesus called 'wild living'.

And yet this is not the end of the story. While the first part of the parable describes some really bad news, at this point in the narrative the whole tenor changes, to good news. Here is how the New International Version Bible translation renders it in verse 20:

> But while he was still a long way off, his father saw him and
> was filled with compassion for him; he ran to his son, threw his
> arms around him and kissed him.

Notice the word 'but'. In the original language of the New Testament (Greek) it's the little word *de*. But even though it may be small in size, it is big in implications. In the word 'but' we have the full glory of what Christians call 'the Gospel', or 'the Good News'. The son had fallen badly, but the father still loved him and ran to him. What an amazing picture!

AMAZING RACE, AMAZING GRACE

A whole wealth of meaning is contained in the word 'ran'. Jesus says, 'He ran to his son.'

First of all, we should note the significance of this word 'ran' *culturally*. Those who are experts in the field tell us that this dad's actions are radical. No man over 30 would run in the culture in which this parable is set. There was a proverb around at the time that went something like this: 'A man's manner of walking tells you what he is.' If a man over 30 was seen running in public it was regarded as a shameful and dishonourable thing. There is a quite practical reason for this. To run meant lifting up the front of your robe, thereby revealing your undergarments. No man who held honour highly would ever do that.

Secondly, we should note the significance of the word 'ran' *emotionally*. The word used here is the Greek word *dremo*, which means to 'race'. The father didn't just jog towards his boy. He didn't even run fast. He sprinted at full pace, in front of many villagers who knew him and his situation all too well. Why did the father sprint? The answer is simple: his feet moved in response to his heart. As we saw in the last chapter, the father had been experiencing endless days and nights of suffering love. When he saw his son returning on this fateful day, he couldn't help himself. He was so filled with compassion that he ran to his boy full-pelt, not holding anything back. Every muscle and sinew was strained to the maximum as he raced to greet his lost child.

Finally, we should note the significance of the word 'ran' *spiritually*. In moral terms, the son had done a dishonourable thing. The villagers would have gathered as this unkempt boy made his way through the village to his father's house. No doubt the locals would have poured scorn on him, increasing the shame. They may even have spat at him and hit him. But the father, anticipating this, ran out to the son before he entered the village. Because of this, the son enters the village under the protection of the father's love. The father's amazing race pointed to his amazing grace. It was his way of saying, 'He doesn't deserve it, but I forgive him.'

THE RUNNING FATHER

Before we look at what this tells us about our Heavenly Father, I want to spend a few moments reflecting on the cover of this book.

The painting on the cover is by one of the most talented Christian artists today, Charlie Mackesey. Charlie has painted two versions of this picture. The first portrays a boy being held in the arms of his father. We have an original oil painting of that picture in the glass porch of our church, St Andrew's, Chorleywood, 5ft by 5ft in size. I was so captivated by the picture when I first saw it that I commissioned Charlie to paint one for us. The first thing people see as they enter our church is this great picture of the father welcoming his son home. It is our way of saying, 'Everyone's welcome here. The Father's arms are open very wide.'

The second version of the picture shows a daughter being held by her father. It is the same picture in every way except for the gender of the child who is being held and the angle of the father's gaze. In every other aspect the painting is identical. One of the main reasons I wanted this version of the picture on the front cover is because daughters as well as sons need to know the perfect love of our Heavenly Father. This book isn't just for men; it's for women too. The cover picture is intended to send that signal in the strongest possible way.

One of the reasons why I chose this picture for the cover is because of the writing over the two figures depicted. If you look closely you can see that Charlie has painted some words in black. This is how they read: 'This is the story of the prodigal daughter. It should really be called the running father – who waits every day for his girl to return, the girl who had rejected him so badly.'

I believe that Charlie has identified something very significant here. He has seen that the real hero of the parable is the father. And he has also spotted that the critical moment is when the father, seeing his son from a distance, ran *to* his son, not from him.

THAT'S ONE DEDICATED FATHER

I love watching and commenting on movies, something I find myself doing more and more. A particularly favourite hobby is looking at the spiritual meaning and message in contemporary films. My friend J.John and I have recently written a book on this subject entitled *A Passion for the Movies* (also published by Authentic Media).

If you were to ask which animated film is my all-time favourite, I would have to say it's *Finding Nemo*. This film tells the story of a little clownfish called Nemo. At the start of the film his father Marlin and his mother Coral are doting on their unborn children, all in little eggs about to hatch. Suddenly, into the idyllic paradise of the coral reef a barracuda strikes, killing the mother (a rather frequent motif in Disney cartoons) and eating all the eggs, bar one – Nemo. Nemo grows up and his father tries his very best to look after him.

But the father, still traumatised by the loss of his wife and children, is overly protective. On his first day at school, Nemo rebels. He disobeys his father and swims beyond the reef to touch a boat on the surface of the sea. As he taunts his over-anxious dad, Nemo is caught in the net of a diver and taken onto the boat, which then leaves for Sydney Harbour. Nemo is imprisoned in a fish tank in the diver's surgery, where he joins a motley crew of very eccentric fish.

The father, in desperate agony, races after his son as fast as he can. But the boat is too quick for him. So he teams up with another fish called Dory, who suffers from acute short-term memory loss, and they go to extreme measures to find

Nemo. They confront three hungry sharks, numerous jellyfish, a huge whale and an assortment of other dangers, before Marlin eventually rediscovers and rescues his son. Just before that happens, a pelican called Nigel tells Nemo what his dad has been doing.

Here is the dialogue:

NIGEL: You see, kid, after you were taken by diver Dan over there, your dad followed the boat you were on like a maniac.

NEMO: Really?

NIGEL: He's swimming and he's swimming and he's giving it all he's got and then three gigantic sharks capture him and he blows them up! And then dives thousands of feet and gets chased by a monster with huge teeth! He ties this demon to a rock and what does he get for a reward? He gets to battle an entire jellyfish forest! And now he's riding with a bunch of sea turtles on the East Australian Current and the word is he's headed this way right now, to Sydney!

Marlin raced through many difficulties to relocate his rebellious son. Nemo didn't deserve this kind of love. But his father gave it anyway. It was his way of saying, 'I don't want to lose you. I forgive you. Come on home.' As another character in the movie puts it, 'That's one dedicated father!'

So What?

You may never have had a dad who loved you so. You may never have had a dad who felt for you, who ran to you when you were in trouble. If present social trends are anything to go by, it's rather unlikely that you have a dedicated dad who is physically and emotionally present. It's unlikely that you have a dad you could run to when you're in trouble, or, even better, who would run to you. So many people in this fatherless society have never known such love. This is bad news indeed.

But there is good news, and the good news is that there is a Father in heaven who loves us with such dedication. By painting this picture of the father in the parable in Luke chapter 15, Jesus was saying something immensely significant to us. He was saying God is a Father who runs to sinful people, even though they rebelled against him and deserve nothing.

One of my favourite Bible verses is in Saint Paul's letter to the Romans (i.e. the Christians in Rome, during the first century). In chapter 5, verses 6–8, he wrote:

When we were utterly helpless, Christ came at just the right time and died for us sinners. Now, no one is likely to die for a good person, though someone might be willing to die for a person who is especially good. But God showed his great love for us by sending Christ to die for us while we were still sinners.

What is Saint Paul saying here? He is talking about a moment in history, two thousand years ago, when we were far away from God. In fact, Saint Paul says we were 'utterly helpless'. The word could also be translated 'at our weakest, at our lowest ebb'. At the very moment when we were furthest away, the Father took the initiative. Even though we had sinned by deciding to reject and neglect him, the Father decided to act. He showed his great love for us by sending his one and only Son to die the death that we deserved. And he did this 'while we were still sinners'.

We can hear echoes here of the parable of parables. As Jesus said, 'While he was still a long distance away, his father saw him coming. Filled with love and compassion, he ran to his son.' However, there is a difference. While in the parable the father himself comes to the rebellious son, in Saint Paul's words we learn that the Father sent his one and only Son. At a time when we were still far away from the Father because of our sins, Jesus Christ came to us and died the death that our sins deserved. In his letter to the Ephesians (chapter 2, verse 13) Saint Paul put it this way:

Though you once were far away from God, now you have been brought near to him because of the blood of Christ.

When we were far away, Jesus died in our place, and as a result, we have been restored to the Father.

THE FATHER'S LIFELINE

The truth that Jesus was conveying in the parable of parables is simply this: God is a Father who runs to rescue us. He is truly the God who saves.

A minister in a church in America was about to start his sermon during an evening service when he briefly introduced a visiting minister in the congregation. He said that the visitor was one of his dearest friends and accordingly asked him to say a few words. With that, an elderly man walked to the pulpit and told a story:

A father, his son, and a friend of his son were sailing off the Pacific coast when a fierce storm hit them and the three were swept into the sea as the boat capsized. Grabbing a rescue line, the father had to make the most painful decision of his life. Who was he to throw the lifeline to? The father knew his own son was a Christian and that the son's friend was not.

The father yelled, 'I love you' to his boy as he threw the line to the boy's friend, pulling him to safety, while his son disappeared for ever beneath the waves. The father knew his son would step into eternity with Jesus but couldn't bear the thought of the friend stepping into an eternity without Jesus. Therefore he sacrificed his son to save the son's friend.

Concluding, the visitor said, 'How great is the Father's love for us that he gave his only Son that we should be rescued. So take hold of the lifeline that the Father is throwing you in this service tonight.'

With that the old man finished and the minister took his place in the pulpit, and preached his message.

At the end of the meeting, some teenagers came up to the visitor. They had been looking very sceptical throughout the old man's story and had not responded to the appeal. 'That wasn't a very realistic story,' they said mockingly. 'No dad would do that.'

'You've got a point,' said the visitor. 'But I'm standing here tonight to tell you that this story gives me, personally, a great glimpse into the Father's love for us. You see, I was that father, and your minister here is my son's friend.'

The Willing Sacrifice of the Son

That story gives us an insight into the Father's love. It points to the agonising decision in the heart of God to allow the Son to die in our place. It gives us a glimpse of the suffering love of the Father as he watched his Son die the death that we deserved on the Cross. It gives us an insight into the constant pain in the Father's heart as human beings go on disregarding the Cross and continue to live their lives in ignorance.

But there is one huge difference between the story of the drowning son and the story of Jesus, God's Son. The truth is the son in the story did not choose to die in the place of his friend. He had absolutely no say in the matter. The decision was out of his hands and he died involuntarily, not voluntarily. With Jesus the exact opposite is the case. In heaven, prior to Jesus' birth, the Father and the Son knew exactly what it was going to take to bring us home. The justice of God said that human beings must experience the consequences of their rejection of God, and this meant death – both physically and spiritually. But the love of God said that this could not be left to continue. So, out of this intolerable tension in the heart of God, the Father acted in history. The Father issued a command that one should die for all, and the Son willingly agreed to enter our world and die in our place. This decision was not forced upon Jesus Christ. Rather, the Son chose willingly to demonstrate the Father's love on the Cross, even when we were far away. As Jesus himself said, in John's Gospel chapter 10, verses 17–18:

The Father loves me because I lay down my life that I may have it back again. No one can take my life from me. I lay down my life voluntarily. For I have the right to lay it down when I want to and also the power to take it again. For my Father has given me this command.

'I lay my life down voluntarily,' Jesus says. And he did. On the Cross, Jesus freely chose to die in our place.

KEEPING THE CROSS IN FOCUS

Just occasionally someone misinterprets the Father's role in Jesus' death as abusive. In a culture where tragically some fathers abuse their children physically and sexually, the violent sufferings of Jesus are wrongly interpreted as the Father abusing his Son physically. But this is not at all the case. The Son *voluntarily* laid down his life. Indeed, Jesus in John chapter 10, verses 17-18 said that he had the 'right' to lay it down.

Furthermore, we should remember that the punishment that Jesus bore was inflicted not by the Father but by those who crucified him. The abuse came not from divine but from human hands. This is the point that Mel Gibson was trying to make during the filming of his movie *The Passion of the Christ*. At a critical moment, when the nails are being driven into Jesus' hands, it is Mel Gibson's hand that is photographed hammering the first nail. This was the director's way of demonstrating that it was we who made Christ suffer so. It was our sins that put him there.

Jesus told the story of the prodigal son not only to highlight the human need for homecoming but also to give us a glimpse of God the Father's heart. When the father in the story runs to his lost child, he does so with only one emotion in his heart: compassion. He had every right to be angry, but he chose to love and forgive. Here is goodness indeed.

Not long ago I was in a small art gallery in a town in the western part of Norway. I was the only person in the room at that time and I got talking to the young woman who ran the shop. I started to describe to her my all-time favourite painting – the picture on the cover of this book, by Charlie Mackesey. As I told her about the painting and shared the parable that inspired it, tears began to well up in her eyes. She was not at all religious and was not familiar with the story. But she felt its power and warmed to the image of God presented in the tale. When I asked her how she felt about it she said, 'I have never before experienced such *goodness.*'

'Goodness'. What a great word! This young woman had really seen it. The father in this story is radiant with goodness. And the good news is this: the one whom Jesus asked us to call 'our Father in heaven' is radiant with goodness too. In fact, he is absolutely perfect in every way.

When we think of what happened at the Cross, it is so important that we remember this picture that Jesus himself painted, a picture that gives love the emphasis. At the Cross we see God's love come running towards us, with arms outstretched. Remember the father racing to his son, defusing the power of guilt and shame in the son's life. If we keep that picture at the forefront, the chances are we will keep the Cross in a proper focus, and we ourselves will experience the Father's embrace, the subject of our next chapter.

CHAPTER 5

AFFECTIONATE

He embraced him . . . (Luke's Gospel 15:20).

It is said that Greg Norman is one of the most ice-cold golfers on the circuit. He learned this from his father. 'I used to see my father, getting off a plane or something, and I'd want to hug him,' he said once. 'But he'd only shake my hand.'

Greg Norman was at the 1996 US Masters, golf's most prestigious tournament, when he made these remarks. Norman let a six-shot lead go during the last round, losing to his great rival Nick Faldo.

Faldo hit a fifteen-foot birdie for the winning shot. He then walked towards Norman, who tried to smile, waiting for the customary handshake. Instead, he found himself in a bear hug embrace from Faldo.

As they held each other, Norman began to weep. Later Norman said, 'I wasn't crying because I lost. I've lost a lot of golf tournaments before. I'll lose a lot more. I cried because

I'd never felt that from another man before. I've never had a hug like that in my life.'

THE FATHER'S EMBRACE

We have reached a critical moment in the story of the prodigal son. The father is running towards him. What is going through the son's mind as his father approaches? 'What's he going to say? Will he beat me? Will my father want me back'? All of this and much more must have entered the son's head.

But the father does none of these things. In fact, the father says absolutely nothing to the boy. Instead, he resorts to actions, four of them in all, each one a message in itself. He runs to the boy, he embraces him, he kisses him and he gives him gifts. Truly actions speak louder than words. As Saint John puts it in his first letter, chapter 3, verse 18:

Dear children, let us stop just saying we love each other; let us really show it by our actions.

The father of the prodigal communicates his love through what he does, not through what he says. If you read the original, Jesus says that the father 'fell upon the boy's neck'. What a great picture of the father's fulsome and unreserved embrace. This father is truly an affectionate father. He knows how to express his emotions in an open, pure and demonstrative way.

'I Love You, Little Girl'

Many fathers today are not so overtly affectionate. Maybe their own fathers failed to show their emotions openly, and they then simply perpetuate this toxic, generational trend. Other fathers want to show their love, but don't know how. They cannot find the words to say. They suffer so much from frozen feelings that they cannot demonstrate love to their children. The best they can do is resort to roundabout expressions of commitment, such as gift-giving. Still other fathers start out loving their children, but then experience rejection and end up rejecting their child.

This in fact is what happened to a friend of mine. She tells her story in her own words:

I was a daddy's little girl. Even from being very young I remember a very deep bond between my dad and me. When I was 10 years old my mum left my dad for another man, which devastated my dad. This resulted in lots of things being said and done, one of which was my dad shouting at me to get out of the car when we were in a busy town shopping centre car park, telling me that I looked too much like my mother and that he never wanted to see me again.

Several years later my dad remarried, but unfortunately my stepmother made it very clear that my brother and I were an inconvenience and she did everything she could to drive a wedge between our dad and us.

At the time, I was constantly haunted by the words my dad had said several years earlier. What little faith I still had that my dad loved me, as he had told me so many times when I was younger, was totally destroyed by what appeared to be his complete indifference to the hurt our stepmum was causing us. There is no way he couldn't have known what was going on, and the fact that he never once stood up for us or spoke about what was happening seemed to confirm to me once and for all that what love we had once shared was totally gone, and in fact I began to doubt that he had ever really loved me at all. So in order to try to get some of my dad's attention back I rebelled.

When I was 20 years old I became a Christian, and during a time of singing worship songs I met my Heavenly Father for the first time. Since that day I have been seeking to know my Father in heaven more and more. I have been travelling the long journey of forgiving and mending what has been broken.

After I became a Christian my relationship with my dad gradually improved, but I was still caught in the same cycle of my dad hurting me and me forgiving him.

Five yeas ago my stepmum died of cancer and my dad remarried. After he remarried, our relationship improved. But deep down I still carried the feelings of rejection and that nagging doubt about whether my dad really did love me at all.

Several weeks ago Dad gave me a lifestyle magazine which he had picked up on one of his trips with his new wife. She had pointed out to Dad a story a few pages from the back of the magazine. The story was about a dad and his little girl. She told my dad that it made her think of my dad and me, so my dad gave me the magazine so I too could read the story.

This is how the story went:

Once upon a time, there was a great man who married the woman of his dreams. With their love, they created a little girl. She was a bright and cheerful little girl and the great man loved her very much.

When she was very little, he would pick her up, hum a tune and dance with her round the room, and he would tell her, 'I love you, little girl.' When the little girl was growing up, the great man would hug her and tell her, 'I love you, little girl.'

The little girl would pout and say, 'I'm not a little girl any more.' Then the man would laugh and say, 'But to me, you will always be my little girl.'

The little girl who was not so little any more left her home and went into the world. As she learned more about herself, she learned more about the man.

She saw that he truly was great and strong, for now she recognised his strengths. One of his strengths was his ability to express his love to his family. It didn't matter where she went in the world, the man would call her and say, 'I love you, little girl.'

The day came when the little girl who was not so little any more received a phone call. The great man was damaged. He had had a stroke, they explained to the little girl. He couldn't talk any more and they weren't sure he could understand the words spoken to him. He could no longer smile, laugh, walk, hug, dance or tell the little girl who wasn't so little any more that he loved her.

And so she went to the side of the great man. When she walked into the room and saw him, he looked small and not strong at all. He looked at her and tried to speak, but he could not.

The little girl did the only thing she could do. She climbed up on to the bed next to the great man. Tears ran from both their eyes and she drew her arms around the useless shoulders of her father.

Her head on his chest, she thought of many things. She remembered the wonderful times together and how she had always felt protected and cherished by the great man. She felt grief for the loss she was to endure, the words of love that had comforted her.

And then she heard from within the man the beat of his heart. The heart where the music and the words had always lived. The heart beat on steadily, unconcerned about the damage to the rest of the body.

And while she rested there, the magic happened. She heard what she needed to hear. His heart beat out the words his mouth could no longer say . . .

I love you, I love you, I love you. Little girl, little girl, little girl.

And she was comforted.

The thing is, my dad never said anything else. . . . He didn't comment on whether the story had meant anything to him . . . but he didn't need to because as soon as I began to read the story the Holy Spirit began to work on my heart. He made me see that my dad did love me and always had loved me. That my dad was, in fact, like the man in the story. The man in the story was physically damaged, whereas my dad is spiritually and emotionally damaged. So even though my dad hasn't been able to tell me he loves me, his heart still beats out the words, 'I love you, little girl.'

As the days and weeks have gone on since reading this story my heavenly dad has showed me stuff about our relationship as well. Before reading this story I would have said I was 100 per cent certain that God loved me and that I didn't need to do anything to obtain his love. However, as God began to unpack this story with me, he showed me that just as I doubted my earthly dad's love deep down, I doubted his love too. That I was really living in fear that one day my heavenly dad would turn around and say, 'I don't love you any more.'

I really can say hand on heart that I will never ever be the same again. It so amazes me and I am lost for words when I try to comprehend how much my heavenly dad loves me, that he would come running to embrace me when I was still 'a long way off'.

SO WHAT?

The picture of the father embracing the prodigal son is critical for understanding what God is really like. It shows us that God is the Father who loves us for who we are, not what we do, the Father who is not afraid of open displays of affection.

When a person becomes a Christian, they choose to put their trust in the person of Jesus Christ and in what he did for us on the Cross. A Christian is someone who follows Jesus. A Christian is someone who believes that Jesus is risen from the dead and alive for evermore. A Christian is accordingly someone who engages in an eternal friendship with the person of Jesus Christ. This means worshipping him with other believers in the public place, and it means worshipping him on one's own in the private place. A Christian is truly a person who loves and obeys Jesus.

But this alone is not enough. Jesus did not come into the world to draw attention to himself. He came to show us the Father and to provide a way back to the Father. Jesus came into the world because the Father sent him, and the Father sent him because he could see that human beings were spiritual orphans living 'home alone' in the universe. Jesus therefore came to reveal the Father. He came to show us that the One who created the universe and who flung stars into space is the Father we've been waiting for all our lives, the perfect Father indeed.

This is why the parable of the prodigal son is the parable of parables. It is the premier parable. It is a story, yes, but it is also a rich resource of revelation concerning the Father's love. In this story, Jesus drops divine hints about the true nature of God. He shows us a Father who is watching intently over his creation, longing for his lost children to come home. He shows us a Father who looks with great compassion on sinners like you and me when we decide to turn round and return home to his arms of love. He shows us a Father who runs towards us when we turn towards him. And he shows us a Father who embraces us when we return to him, who falls upon our necks and weeps with joy over our homecoming.

So to be a Christian is to be a follower of Jesus, yes. But to be a Christian is also to be a child of the perfect Father. It is to be a son or a daughter of the Living God by adoption.

It is to know Jesus, yes, but it is also to know the Father, in the fullest, most experiential and affectionate way. A Christian is someone who has come home to the Father of all fathers.

INTRODUCING THE HOLY SPIRIT

How then can we know the Father's love in our hearts? The key here is to understand who the Holy Spirit is and what the Holy Spirit does.

The Holy Spirit is first of all personal. Most people, if they think about the Holy Spirit at all, think about some kind of force field of energy or some kind of ghostly presence. But the Bible clearly shows that the Holy Spirit is personal. When Jesus talks about the Holy Spirit he uses the personal pronoun 'he'. He refers to the Holy Spirit as divine and as personal. In fact, listening to what Jesus says, you realise that the Holy Spirit is part of the Godhead. The Godhead comprises three persons who share in the one essence or being. These three persons are described as 'Father, Son and Holy Spirit'. While it is easy for us to conceive of the Father and the Son in personal terms, it is not so easy in the case of the Holy Spirit. We have to remind ourselves constantly that the Spirit of God is his personal presence among us.

Secondly, the Holy Spirit is powerful. When the Holy Spirit comes upon God's people, there is always a powerful manifestation of that presence. In Acts chapter 2, the Holy

Spirit falls upon the 120 followers of Jesus who have gathered in Jerusalem for the Day of Pentecost. They have been told by Jesus to wait for the coming of the Holy Spirit. When the Holy Spirit does come, he comes like a mighty rushing wind and he fills the 120 disciples with his powerful presence. They respond by speaking in unlearned foreign languages about how great God is. This is not some manic behaviour but a miraculous manifestation of the Holy Spirit. These 120 followers of Jesus were surrounded by people of many different nationalities who had come to Jerusalem for the festival. When the Holy Spirit filled the disciples, they were given the supernatural ability to communicate with these people in tongues they hadn't learned by natural means.

So there are two things we need to remember about the Holy Spirit. First, he is personal – indeed, a divine person, part of the One-in-Three. Secondly, he is powerful. He is God's presence in great strength.

EXPERIENCING THE FATHER'S EMBRACE

How then can we know the Father's love *experientially*? The answer is by the Holy Spirit. In other words, we need to become a Christian and becoming a Christian involves two things – believing in Jesus and what he has done for us on the Cross, and receiving the Holy Spirit in our hearts. Believing and receiving: these are the keys to becoming a Christian and experiencing the Father's love.

Why is the Holy Spirit so important? The Bible gives us the answer. In the fifth chapter of his letter to the Romans, Saint Paul says this in verse 5:

For we know how dearly God loves us, because he has given us the Holy Spirit to fill our hearts with his love.

In these words, Saint Paul makes it clear that the heartfelt knowledge of the Father's love comes only by the work of the Holy Spirit. The Holy Spirit is the fire of God's love. If we are to experience the Father's embrace in our lives, we must have that fire burning in the hearth of our hearts.

In another passage in the same letter, Saint Paul talks about the way the Holy Spirit shows us that we are the adopted children of God, and how he inspires us to cry out 'Dear Father' in our worship of God. Here is how he puts it in chapter 8, verses 15–16:

So you should not be like cowering, fearful slaves. You should behave instead like God's very own children, adopted into his family – calling him 'Father, dear Father'. For his Holy Spirit speaks to us deep in our hearts and tells us that we are God's children.

From these two passages alone we can see that the Holy Spirit is absolutely critical if we are to experience the

Father's embrace. If we want to know the Father's love in our hearts, we must not only believe in Jesus, we must also receive the Holy Spirit.

SID'S STORY

Not long ago I was speaking on this subject at a conference in Canada. That night there was a man in his mid-sixties called Sid in the audience. He had decided to come along that evening but he didn't want to sit near anyone. He just wanted to be alone and listen, so he found a place in the auditorium where no one else was sitting and took a seat there.

In the middle of my talk about the Father's love, Sid closed his eyes and put his head in his hands. I could see him but I had no idea what was happening in his life. At the end of the talk I invited people to come forward and receive prayer with the laying-on of hands. I particularly wanted to pray for people that night to experience the Father's love in their hearts.

As I was walking around the front of the stage praying for people, I noticed Sid sitting with his back to the stage, sobbing. I went and sat next to him and asked him who he was and why he was crying. He told me that he had experienced something wonderful in the middle of my talk. As I had been speaking he had suddenly felt big, strong arms wrap themselves around his shoulders. Immediately he had opened his eyes and looked around, but he could see that there was no one there. He thought it strange but then closed his eyes again. Immediately he felt strong and affectionate arms embracing him. This time he opened his eyes more quickly. Again, no one was there. So a third and final time he closed his eyes. This time he knew what it was. As he felt the embrace again, he knew it was the Father's arms of love and he began to weep.

Sid told me his dad had died sixty years before, when Sid was five years old. He had never known a dad's hug all his life. But that night, as he heard about the love of his Heavenly Father, the Holy Spirit fell upon him and he experienced the divine embrace of God. He felt the sacred touch of the father he'd been longing for all his life.

As he left the conference that night he said to me, 'I'm going back to my church this weekend, and I'm going to tell them all that God is relational, not remote.'

ARMS OF LOVE

Like the young woman whose story I shared a few pages back, Sid experienced the personal and powerful touch of the Holy Spirit. He felt the Father's divine embrace and he will never be the same again.

This is why the Holy Spirit is so important if we are to know the Father we've been waiting for. In a great passage in the Book of Acts in the New Testament, Saint Peter is preaching to a household of people who are neither Jewish (as Peter was) nor Christians. As he shares all about Jesus with them, the following happens (you can read it in verses 44–45 of chapter 10):

Even as Peter was saying these things, the Holy Spirit fell upon all who had heard the message. The Jewish believers who came with Peter were amazed that the gift of the Holy Spirit had been poured out upon the Gentiles, too.

The thing that I find most interesting about this story is the way in which the writer says that the Holy Spirit 'fell upon' those who heard the message. The writer here is Saint Luke. He not only wrote the Book of Acts, but also wrote the Gospel which bears his name. This means that he is the one who recorded the story Jesus told about the prodigal son, which is found only in Luke's Gospel. Why is this important? It is important because the father in the parable is said to have 'embraced' the son, and the word 'embraced' can be translated 'he fell upon' his son. This is exactly what happens to Peter's audience in Acts 10.

This speaks to me of one of the primary functions of the Holy Spirit. The Holy Spirit falls upon those who believe in Jesus, so that they will experience the affectionate embrace of God. Just as the father fell upon the prodigal son in the story, so the Father falls upon us today in the person of the Spirit. He does this so that we may experience his embrace not just as an idea in our heads but as a reality in our hearts. The hallmark of the Holy Spirit is love, and it is by this Holy Spirit that we are overwhelmed with divine love, as Sid was.

The lasting lesson of all this is that the father in the parable is a dad who goes for embrace rather than exclusion. As the great nineteenth-century preacher Charles Spurgeon once put it:

> God on the neck of a sinner! What a wonderful picture! Can you conceive it? I do not think you can; but if you cannot imagine it, I hope that you will realize it. When God's arm is about our neck, and his lips are on our cheek, kissing us much, then we understand more than preachers or books can ever tell us of his . . . love.

My conviction is that anyone can experience the affectionate embrace of the Father. This is not a privilege reserved for the select few. Everyone who truly seeks God with all their heart will surely find him. That is the promise of the Bible. That is also my experience. If you are sincerely seeking after God, why not ask him right now to reveal himself to you as your loving, affectionate Father? Ask him to show himself to you in a way that you cannot mistake. And ask in the name of Jesus, the one who revealed that 'the Father himself loves you dearly' (John 16:27).

Chapter 6

Intimate

And he kissed him . . . (Luke's Gospel 15:20).

A Christian leader called Joe Bayly – a gentle, loving man – once told the story of how one of his sons rebelled in the days of the hippie movement. The boy did all the things that hippies used to do and moved into a communal house.

Late one night, Joe received a phone call in which he was told that his son had been arrested and was being held at a police station. Joe got out of bed, dressed and drove round to the police station, only to find that his boy wasn't there. They had no record of him. Confused, Joe then drove to the other local police stations and heard the same story.

Eventually Joe realised that he had been the victim of a hoax call. By now it was 2 a.m. and he was very tired. But before he went home he decided to visit the communal house where he now knew his son would be sleeping. He went in and stepped over sleeping bodies, until he found his boy seemingly asleep on the floor. He gently bent over and kissed his son goodnight, then went home to his own bed.

The son shortly afterwards became a Christian and later became a church leader himself. Years later he was to ask his father Joe, 'Dad, do you know what turned me around and brought me home?'

Joe replied, 'No, son.'

'It was the night you came into my room at the house and kissed me. You thought I was asleep but I wasn't. I figured to myself, "If my dad loves me that much, then I had better get my life right with God." So that's what I did.'

Such is the power of a father's tender, pure and loving kiss.

It is a reminder to parents of how important it is to display affection towards their children.

THE DEMONSTRATIVE FATHER

In the parable of the prodigal son, we read that the father not only embraced his boy, he also kissed him. In fact, the word 'kissed' represents the last in a rush of verbs here. In quick succession the dad is described as seeing, then running, then embracing, before finally kissing. The act of kissing his son is the climactic moment in a welcome that involves no words at all.

To a Jewish audience (the original audience Jesus was speaking to) the father's behaviour would have been regarded as radical. At every turn he surprises us with his outrageous grace.

In the final action of the father we see yet another surprise. Jesus says the father 'kissed' his boy. That is a rather lame translation of what is said in the original Greek. The full force of this word is 'kissed repeatedly, tenderly and earnestly'.

Why is this kiss such a surprise? There are three reasons.

First, it is surprising because by rights the son should have fallen at his father's feet and kissed them in an open demonstration of his repentance. We will never know if he was intending to do that: the father got there first. He fell on his boy's neck and kissed his son over and over again. I am sure that he soaked his son's dirty, matted hair with his tears.

Secondly, it is surprising because in the culture concerned, such a kiss could mean only one thing, that the father was now reconciled to his son. When two disputing parties came to be reconciled, they would seal their new unity with a public display of affection like this. It was a social convention of the day. The public kiss of the father was his way of saying to the accusing villagers, 'We have made it up.'

Thirdly, it is surprising because the father doesn't know whether his son is repentant. He embraces and kisses his boy *unconditionally*. The mere fact that he has come home is enough to justify this uninhibited display of undeserved love. Whether or not the boy is sorry for his wrongdoing is irrelevant to the father at this point.

A PARENT'S TOUCH

This kind of extraordinarily intimate parental behaviour is extremely rare in most western cultures today.

Many children have never known the holy, loving touch of a father. So many live with what has been called 'tactile deprivation'. To quote the title of a movie, too many children have simply 'never been kissed'. And the consequences psychologically and spiritually have been devastating.

Psychiatrist René Spitz conducted a study of the importance of parental affection. Spitz went to a South American orphanage and studied what happened to 97 children who were starved of physical affection and contact. These children were 3 months to 3 years old. The study was conducted in an environment where shortage of staff meant that the nurses only changed nappies and fed the children, nothing more. At no point did they hold, cuddle and talk to them in the way a mother or a father would.

After three months, many of these children started to show abnormal behaviour. Some lost their appetites, others found it hard to sleep, and many just lay on their beds with a vacant stare. After five months, the deterioration became even more disturbing. The children lay crying, with troubled and twisted looks on their faces. Whenever they were picked up, they would scream in fear.

In the first year, almost one-third of the children died, but not from lack of healthcare or nutrition. They died from tactile deprivation, or a lack of touch and emotional warmth. Seven more died in the second year for the same reasons. Only 21 of the original 97 children survived, but most of these suffered severe emotional traumas and lasting psychological damage.

Few studies show the effects of the lack of a parent's touch more graphically than this one. The truth is, many children today live like these children. They do not enjoy appropriate, physical intimacy with their parents, especially with their fathers. Consequently, many grow up into adulthood with a huge love deficit.

PAULINE'S STORY

A woman called Pauline wrote to me recently about her experiences as a child. She is now in her sixties. In her childhood she experienced physical abuse rather than intimacy at the hands of her father. This is her story:

It all started with World War Two. My father was in the Tank Corps. He was a Desert Rat. Like many others at the time, he had some horrendous experiences. These meant that he came out of the war crippled with arthritis and in a bad state of mental health. He started to drink for two reasons: to deaden the memories and to help take away the excruciating pain from the arthritis.

He spent morning, noon and night in a public house and my mother was ordered to go with him, so as children, my sister and I would sit on the step outside the door of the public bar in the rain, snow or whatever the weather. Children were not allowed to go into public houses in those days, but we could ask anyone who was going into the bar to ask my father for lemonade and crisps. This continued until my father seriously embarrassed my mother in front of his friends and she refused to go with him any more.

As the drinking increased, he vented his anger on my mother, my sister and me. He would beat my mother with anything he could get hold of, but usually he used a broom, very often around the head, which caused a lot of blood to be shed. I do not recall exactly how many times the police came to our door at the instigation of the neighbours, but there were many, many occasions. When asked by the police, however, my mother always said that everything was OK.

So the violence increased, with furniture being broken and plates with dinner on them thrown against walls, and it was always my job to clear up the mess. On one occasion – and these were always in the evening after my father came home from the pub – he pushed my head through a glass window-pane. My father was never repentant, because the next day he could not remember what he had done.

My school friends used to talk in a mocking way about 'the alcoholic' who used to walk around with a stick and dark glasses, falling into hedges etc., and I was ashamed and embarrassed in case anyone found out that I was his daughter and where I lived.

Because my mother was afraid of my father, in my late teens I was never allowed to return home after my father had come in, which was usually around 10 o'clock. Hence, if I went to the cinema and the bus would not get me home until 10 p.m., I would have to sleep that night on a park bench.

I was now 18. With my sister having long since emigrated to Canada and with a much younger brother to worry about, I began to wonder if there were any life ahead for me. Was there anything outside this life? I had developed a hatred for men, as I had assumed that all men were like my father.

My mother worked to make up for the money my father spent on drinking, which meant that I had to do the cooking, cleaning and gardening and I also had the responsibility for my brother. This sometimes seemed too much and gave me little time for socialising.

Then came the evening when my father came home, drunk as usual, and I was in bed asleep. I remember being woken up by a pillow being put over my face and feeling my father's heavy body across mine. My mother was screaming and trying to pull my father off me, and the pillow from my face, but thankfully, when I was on the point of passing out, my father collapsed in a drunken stupor. Although I did not realise it at the time, I am sure that this was God working on my behalf.

I'd had enough and I made plans to end my life. I caught a bus to Harrow with every intention of throwing myself in front of a train. I had considered that this was probably the quickest way to end all the pain that I was going through.

There was a gang of Teddy boys at the corner of the main road, however, so I turned down a side street, this being a short cut to the station. Suddenly a man tapped me on the shoulder.

I thought I was being attacked, but when I turned round, this man told me that Jesus loved me. There was no way that I could accept this, because I could not understand how anyone could love me. However, the man kept on saying that Jesus loved me. This man gave me the Gospel message and told me that if I trusted Jesus with my life, my Father in heaven would never leave me nor forsake me.

Hope started to rise in me. Could it be possible that God loved me that much and would have a purpose for my life? I decided to take the chance and knelt down on the pavement and gave my life to Jesus. After I had prayed the prayer, I felt as if warm oil were being poured over my head and running down the inside of my body and also on the outside.

I got up, and had such joy in my heart and felt as if I loved everybody in the world. I returned home and at the first opportunity I told my mother. She assured me that it would not last. That was forty-five years ago: she was wrong!

My mother herself became a Christian a little while later. She went to be with the Lord seven years ago and then I had to face forgiving my father, who had died in 1979. I found such a release and a love when I forgave him, even though he was not there, and I found that I could then understand what had brought him to become an alcoholic.

Five months after becoming a Christian I met Peter, now my husband, and I learned that most men were not at all like my dad. I also came to know my heavenly Father's unconditional love. He loves me as no earthly father ever could. It has been so liberating to know that.

Such stories are typical today. I have listened so many times to adults who never knew the kind of parental affection we see in the father in the parable. Far too many have never known a father's intimacy. They have either missed out on it altogether or have only known a perversion of it, in the form of physical or sexual abuse. Such people need to know that their Heavenly Father is not like this at all, and that he's the dad they've been looking and longing for all their lives.

So What?

The Good News of the parable in Luke 15 is that it proves once and for all that our Heavenly Father is not like many earthly fathers. Our Heavenly Father is a loving, affectionate and tender Father who can be trusted. His touch is always kind and pure. His kisses are like the kisses of the father in the parable: they are totally holy and indescribably intimate.

Why is this not made more public?

The reason is because God has been misrepresented by many people. He has been depicted as distant and angry. Many people, having had painful experiences of being fathered, project their own fathers onto God. They transfer their father wounds into their image of God the Father. Consequently they see God as distant, abusive, unreliable, unavailable, critical, rejecting and cold.

But God is a loving Father – the most loving Father in the universe. Wherever you are on your spiritual journey, his desire is that you come home and experience his affectionate embrace. He wants you to know that he is not like many earthly fathers, that he is always there for you and that you can trust him 100 per cent.

A friend of mine called Lindsay came to realize this. Here is her brief story:

I was brought up by a father who adored my sister but ignored me. He used to say that I was not even his child, that someone else was the father. In my forties I gave my life to Jesus Christ and went to two Spirit-filled friends to ask them to pray for me. As they did so, the Holy Spirit came upon me in such a powerful way that I had to kneel down on the floor. Then the man (who knew nothing of my past) had a prophetic word for me: 'You have a father who thinks that you are not his child. But your Heavenly Father wants you to know that you are his child, and that he loves you dearly.'

As you can imagine, these words had a profound effect on my life. For the first time I could relate to God as Father! I was filled with a deep sense of assurance about my worth in the Father's eyes.

THE SEARCH FOR INTIMACY

God created us with a need to be loved, a need for intimacy. Until we let the Father fill our hearts with his love, there will always be a love deficit in our lives. We will always seek in other people what we can only find in the Father.

There is a story in the Gospels that highlights this truth. In chapter 4 of John's Gospel, Jesus meets a Samaritan woman at a well outside a town. They get into conversation. Jesus talks to her about her greatest need, for the 'living water' that is far more satisfying than the water in the well (by this Jesus means the Holy Spirit). She expresses her interest and he tells her to go and fetch her husband.

At this point the woman confesses that she doesn't have a husband and Jesus tells her that she is telling the truth: she has had no fewer than five husbands and the man she is now living with is not her husband. She gasps with amazement and recognises that Jesus is a prophet, that he can see things supernaturally. Rather than criticising her for her addiction to relationships, however, he starts talking to her about 'worship'.

Jesus teaches her that there is a Father whom she can worship. The word he uses seven times for worship literally means 'to approach someone in order to kiss them'. Jesus invites the woman to seek from God that which she has so far been searching for in men. Excited by this offer, she runs back to town to fetch everyone she can find to meet this amazing man, Jesus of Nazareth. Her search for intimacy is now over. She had been worshipping men when she could have been worshipping the Father. Now, in the tender embrace of the Loving Father, her quest for love is over.

And it can be over for you and me as well. Many of us are like the woman in this story. We have a big cavity in our lives and we seek to fill it in the wrong ways. But Jesus doesn't want us to worship people or things. He wants us to worship the Father. He wants us to approach the Father and kiss him. When we do, we will find that he has already run to kiss us!

THE KISS OF GOD

One hundred years ago, in 1904–5, there was a great
Christian revival in Wales. During that revival, the favourite
hymn was 'Here is Love, Vast as the Ocean'. This hymn was all
about the Cross of Christ. The second verse reads as follows:

On the mount of crucifixion
Fountains opened deep and wide;
Through the floodgates of God's mercy
Flowed a vast and gracious tide.
Grace and love, like mighty rivers,
Poured incessant from above,
And heaven's peace and perfect justice
Kissed a guilty world in love.

The Father has already kissed a guilty world in love. He has
demonstrated his great love by sending his Son to die for us
on the Cross. Will you accept the kiss of God's forgiveness?
Will you reciprocate by worshipping the Father from this
day on, by approaching him to embrace and kiss him?

Maybe it's time for you to approach the Father in order
to experience the kiss of God. The Bible says, 'Draw close to
God, and God will draw close to you' (James 4:8). He is
longing for relational intimacy with you.

A story is told of a father during the Second World War.
As war broke out in 1939, his wife gave birth to their first

child, a son. Not long afterwards, the father went off to fight in the war. He was away for more than five years.

During that time the child grew up without ever knowing his father personally. His mother, trying to keep his dad's memory alive, would engage in a ritual every evening at bedtime. She would say prayers with her child and then invite her son to kiss Daddy goodnight. A photograph of his father stood on the mantelpiece on the other side of the bedroom. The boy would get out of bed, walk across the floor, climb onto a chair and then kiss the photograph of his father.

After the end of the war the dad eventually came home. The boy was now 5 or 6 years old and there was a rather strange and awkward meal with his wife and child on his first evening home. At bedtime the three of them went upstairs and said prayers. The mother, as she had done faithfully for the previous five years, invited her son to kiss her father goodnight. The boy promptly got out of bed, crossed the floor, climbed onto a chair, and kissed the picture.

The lesson?

Don't settle for second-hand religion. Settle for reality and relationship.

I will leave the last word once again with the great preacher Charles Spurgeon. He describes the sight of the father kissing his son in the parable. He concludes with the spiritual implications:

Let me try to describe the scene. The father has kissed the son, and he bids him sit down; then he comes in front of him, and looks at him, and feels so happy that he says, 'I must give you another kiss,' then he walks away a minute; but he is back again before long, saying to himself, 'Oh, I must give him another kiss!' He gives him another, for he is so happy. His heart beats fast; he feels very joyful; the old man would like the music to strike up; he wants to be at the dancing; but meanwhile he satisfies himself by a repeated look at his long-lost child. Oh, I believe that God looks at the sinner, and looks at him again, and keeps on looking at him, all the while delighting in the very sight of him, when he is truly repentant, and comes back to his Father's house.

CHAPTER 7

FORGIVING

His son said to him, 'Father, I have sinned against both heaven and you, and I am no longer worthy of being called your son.' But his father said to the servants, 'Quick! Bring the finest robe in the house and put it on him' (Luke's Gospel 15:21–22).

Reinhold Niebuhr was one of the most respected theologians of the twentieth century. He wrote the famous prayer associated with Alcoholics Anonymous:

God grant me the serenity
to accept the things I cannot change,
Courage to change the things I can,
and wisdom to know the difference.

When Niebuhr was 21 years old, his father died. Two months later, the young man spoke in the pulpit his father used to occupy. This is what he said:

As a child I once spent a day with my grandmother. Toward evening a severe storm began. 'Now how will you get home, child?' she asked. But then my father came to fetch me. He had a big blue coat and as we left he said, 'Come under here.' I slipped under the coat, grabbed his hand, and off we went. I couldn't see anything as we splashed through puddles and mire. I heard the rain and the thunder and seized my father's hand and held it tightly. I would have been a fool if I had complained that it was dark around me. After all, it was my father's coat, protecting me from the weather, that made it dark. Father saw the path; I knew that . . . and when the coat parted, we were home! Father had brought me home. . . .

So it is with our Heavenly Father. If only we trust him, he holds our hand, takes us under his wings and leads us through storm and tempest.

TREATED LIKE A GUEST OF HONOUR

It is a wonderful thing to be under the covering and protection of a good father. Niebuhr knew that as a child and was able to use this for the rest of his life as a springboard for talking about the Father's love. The son in the parable that Jesus told in Luke 15 had this experience too. At his homecoming, his father placed him under the covering and protection of a special robe. To all the servants who had run the race with him, the father said, 'Fetch the robe of honour.'

So what was this robe? The word literally means a long flowing gown. It would have been a very special garment reserved for unique occasions such as festivals. It was also a garment used for visiting dignitaries. If an important guest visited the village, the father would clothe them in this robe as a sign of favour and honour.

The father's action in clothing his son with this robe is immensely significant. The boy would have been extremely dirty and smelly. He had been living with the pigs in a far-off country, even feeding on the carob pods they had to eat in the time of famine. In such a humiliating, unkempt condition the boy would have been in severe danger of further shaming, this time from the waiting villagers who knew all too well of his dishonourable behaviour. In the telling words of the poet Adrian Plass, this boy had gone from being affluent to effluent. How was he going to run the gauntlet to his father's house?

He doesn't have to! The father runs it instead of him and, having embraced and kissed him, he then covers the boy's shame in a robe of honour. This robe was the father's way of proclaiming (again without words), 'I have forgiven him.' It took the wind out of the accusers' sails and it made it safe for the boy to come home. Thanks to this robe, the boy experiences an extraordinary exchange. The son receives the father's honour and the father takes the son's shame. Thanks to this robe, the boy now enters the village under the protective care of his father.

THE FATHER'S FORGIVING LOVE

When we try to sum up this extraordinary action in a single word, the word that comes to mind is 'forgiveness'. Jesus often taught about the need to forgive other people. In the prayer known as the Lord's Prayer he urged his followers to say, 'Forgive us our sins, just as we have forgiven those who have sinned against us' (Matthew 6:12). In Matthew 18:21–22, we hear the following exchange between Peter and Jesus:

Then Peter came to him and asked, 'Lord, how often should I forgive someone who sins against me? Seven times?' 'No!' Jesus replied, 'seventy times seven!'

Forgiveness was a frequent theme in the teaching of Jesus. He told his followers to forgive others. Why is it so important to forgive those who have hurt us? The answer is because unforgiveness causes our hearts to grow cold, bitter and resentful. Failure to forgive can lead to serious damage to our spiritual, emotional, mental and even physical health. As Sheila Cassidy – who was imprisoned by the Chilean dictator Pinochet – has said:

However much we have been wronged, however justified our hatred, if we cherish it, it will poison us. Hatred is a devil to be cast out, and we must pray for the power to forgive, for it is in forgiving our enemies that we are healed.

When we look at the father in the parable Jesus told, we see an extraordinary example of forgiveness. He had every right to feel extremely wounded by his son's behaviour. But when the moment of choice arrived, he decided to let go of his rejection and to forgive his son. He decided to give his son a gift he did not deserve: the gift of his forgiveness.

Four things should be noted about this forgiveness.

First of all, it was *instant* forgiveness. The father simply saw his son, had compassion on him, ran to him, embraced him, kissed him and clothed him in a very special robe. He did not make his son earn his forgiveness over a period of time by giving him lots of hurdles to overcome. Rather, he simply forgave him, immediately and unconditionally, no strings attached. That's amazing love!

Secondly, it was *complete* forgiveness. The father did not hold back. He gave total forgiveness to his son. He did not say to his boy, 'I'm forgiving you but I'm not forgetting.' He did not engage in half-hearted forgiveness. Nor did he claim to forgive but resolve in the future to mention the boy's former sins if he ever stepped out of line. Rather, he forgave him completely. It brings to mind the story of Clara Barton, founder of the American Red Cross. She was reminded one day of a vicious deed that someone had done to her years before, but she acted as if she had never even heard of the incident. 'Don't you remember it?' her friend asked. 'No,' came Barton's reply, 'I distinctly remember forgetting it.' Again − like the father in the parable − that signifies complete forgiveness. And that's an example of amazing love!

Thirdly, it was *sacrificial* forgiveness. To forgive the boy cost the father. It cost him to let go of his son when the son rejected him. It cost the father to receive him back when the son came home. No one ever said it is easy to forgive those who have wounded us. Forgiveness hurts. Again, that's amazing love!

Fourthly, it was *restorative* forgiveness. Not only did the father forgive his son, he also restored his boy to the relationship he had enjoyed before. As we will see in the next chapter, the father not only gave him a robe, he gave him a ring. Both gifts were the father's way of saying, 'You are restored to your position as my son. Our relationship is healed. Welcome back.' Again, that's amazing love.

SO WHAT?

In the single image of the robe of honour, covering the boy's shame, we are taken right back to the Garden of Eden. In the first three chapters of the Bible we read of the disobedience of Adam and Eve. Whether you regard these two individuals literally or symbolically is really irrelevant here. The fact is, their behaviour was typically human. Having heard what God's boundaries are, they gave in to the temptation to transgress them. They ate the fruit that was forbidden. To put it in the language of the Bible, they 'sinned'. They chose self-rule rather than the rule of God.

After this rebellion, Adam and Eve suddenly noticed that they were naked and they felt ashamed. In Genesis chapter 3, verse 21, after issuing punishments for all those involved in this act of disobedience, the Father showed his mercy. We read that he made clothes out of animal skins for both Adam and his wife, so that their shame was covered.

In the rest of the pages of the Old Testament, we see God's people seeking atonement – a way of becoming 'at one' with God again. In his mercy, the Father provides a system of sacrifices designed to help people experience forgiveness. These are designed to cover human sinfulness. Indeed, the word 'atonement' in Hebrew is *kaphar*, which means 'covering'. Most notably, God instigates the Passover festival at the time of his people's great escape from Egypt. He stipulates that once a year an unblemished male lamb will be taken by the father of every Jewish household and presented to the priests. The lamb will be sacrificed and its blood will be shed for the sins of that household and indeed the people of Israel. Thanks to that shed blood, the Angel of

Death would pass over (hence Passover) God's people and they would be covered, protected against divine judgment.

Thankfully, this system did not continue for ever. As we saw in Chapter 2, the Father waited until a specific moment in history and sent his Son. When John the Baptist saw Jesus, he proclaimed:

'Look! There is the Lamb of God who takes away the sin of the world!' (John 1:29).

Jesus, like the Passover lamb, was perfect and unblemished. He was tempted as human beings are but he never gave in. On the Cross, the sinless Son of God died as the Lamb of God, as our perfect substitute. Thanks to his death, those who believe in Jesus receive forgiveness for all their sins. And this forgiveness is *instant* (the moment we repent), *complete* (God forgives and forgets), *sacrificial* (it cost God everything) and *restorative* (it reconciles us to God). Like the father's forgiveness in the parable, our Heavenly Father's forgiveness is the ultimate demonstration of his amazing love. God gave us a gift we don't deserve – forgiveness. All we have to do is repent and believe.

So, from now on, we who were once far away from God and covered in shame are covered by a robe of righteousness we never could have earned. This is the great truth proclaimed by church leader Martin Luther (1483–1546) in the time of the Reformation in the sixteenth century. He saw very clearly that we cannot get right with God through good works. Our good works are like 'filthy rags' (Isaiah 64:6). However, on the Cross, Jesus has done everything we need to make us right before God. All we have to do is believe in the finished work of the Cross. Then we can be 'justified' or 'declared righteous' before God by faith. We can say with the prophet Isaiah, 'I am overwhelmed with joy in the LORD my God! For he has dressed me with the clothing of salvation and draped me in a robe of righteousness' (Isaiah 61:10).

As Luther saw, thanks to the Cross we have a new set of spiritual clothes. We have a royal robe of righteousness given by the Father and belonging to his One and Only Son. Those who believe in Jesus, who receive the forgiveness Jesus won for us at the Cross, receive the same great deal that the prodigal son received. We get God's honour and he gets our shame. Now, wearing this robe, clothed with Christ, we are under the Father's protection and can be sure of total forgiveness.

FORGIVING AS YOU ARE FORGIVEN

But there is another lesson to be learned here. Not only must we accept the Father's forgiving love, we must also forgive those who have hurt us. Saint Paul puts it this way in Colossians chapter 3, verses 12–14:

Since God chose you to be the holy people whom he loves, you must clothe yourselves with tender-hearted mercy, kindness, humility, gentleness and patience. You must make allowance for each other's faults and forgive the person who offends you. Remember, the Lord forgave you, so you must forgive others. And the most important piece of clothing you must wear is love. Love is what binds us all together in perfect harmony.

As we put on the new robe of righteousness, we are called to be radical in our loving of others and to forgive others even as we ourselves have been forgiven. Failing to forgive prevents us from fully entering into the all-forgiving love of the Father. As Jesus said, in Mark's Gospel chapter 11, verse 25, 'When you are praying, first forgive anyone against whom you are holding a grudge, so that your Father in heaven will forgive your sins, too.' In these words Jesus makes it very clear that failing to forgive will block our spiritual arteries and prevent us from experiencing the Father's forgiving love in all its fullness. We must become a people of forgiveness.

The story of a friend of mine called Julie shows how vital forgiveness is:

I am going to refer to my biological father as Michael. He suffered severely from manic depression. He was irrational, controlling, unpredictable and self-centred, and had an inability to convey love and approval. He

111

did not know how to control his anger. I was not as academic in my studies as my sister, so encouraging me was not his strong point. Partly because of this, my self-confidence and self-esteem were little to none.

My earliest memories of Michael's behaviour are from when I was 3 years old. Michael's whole stature was overbearing. He was 6ft 4in tall and very broad. His shadow was ever-present in the house, and as a child I had to be seen and not heard. Michael was an ill man. He tried to take his own life on many occasions. Several times I visited him in hospital after he had overdosed on painkillers.

During these tough times I was also physically ill. I was diagnosed with epilepsy at 10. I then began to get a great deal of pain in my knees. At 18 years old I had my first exploratory knee operation. The outcome was that I had the arthritic knees of a 70-year-old. The condition is called Chondromalaciapatella syndrome, which means the back of the kneecap falls apart. My knee was wasting away.

At the same time I developed lactose intolerance, a condition that means my stomach cannot tolerate lactose, the sugar found in cow's milk.

Then there was another blow. At 20 years of age I had cysts on my ovaries and other complications, which meant there was a high risk of not being able to have children. In October 2002, after four months of constant headaches, we finally got to see a consultant neurologist at King's College Hospital in London. I was diagnosed with transformed migraines. They are a rare form of migraine, which feeds off itself. It will never pass unless a particular drug successfully interrupts its cycle. My drugs were not working. I could have suffered from this one headache for the rest of my life.

On 21 March 2003, my husband and I attended a conference called 'The Father Loves You'. On the first evening, about ten minutes into the talk I started to cry. The speaker was talking about forgiveness and freedom. I thought I had forgiven Michael, but I also knew I was holding on to some of the hurt and memories, and dealing with them was going to be too hard. I went to the front with hundreds of other people. I knew God was dealing with a videotape of images in my mind, issues that needed erasing. I knew these issues would begin to affect our marriage if I didn't sort them out.

We were led through a prayer of forgiveness. I forgave Michael for taking my childhood away from me, for abusing his rights as a father, and for every bad memory I had. I felt light, I felt joy, I felt excitement. I wasn't angry; I had the videotape erased – not all the memories, but the feelings associated with the memories. I got rid of twenty-six years' worth of pain. How awesome is that!

Even though I was free emotionally, physically I was still a mess. But God was dealing with this too. I was lying on my back on the floor and heard someone pray, 'Receive your healing from Father God.' My legs began to tingle, I had severe stomach cramps and my head felt like it was going to explode. It was unbearable, yet I was still and peaceful.

But this was not the end. I opened my eyes and remember saying, 'I have no pain.' My knee pain had gone; I could kneel down, which I had not been able to do for years, I could jump up and down without pain, my headaches had gone, and I didn't feel sick. It was incredible.

Once I got home, my knees were still great, and there were no headaches either. I thought it would be good to sneak a couple of cream eggs to see if God had healed my lactose intolerance as well as my legs and headaches! Three times I tried the chocolate, and I had cereal with loads of milk, cheese sandwiches, ice cream: you name it, I tried it. I tried all these foods again, and I still had no effects at all. I was healed!

Anyway, a year and four months on I still have no head pain, can still eat anything that comes from a cow's udder, can still run and exercise, and my epilepsy is now under control. God has set me free physically.

This healing has changed my life, and has also challenged many people around us. People who know us have witnessed our suffering, and they have now witnessed my healing. I can now hear and say the word 'father' without crying. I don't have the same fear of men, and I also enjoy buying a Father's Day card for my father-in-law. Plus I love chocolate and can exercise again!

This has been a tough journey, but also a blessed journey. My life has taught me so much, and I can witness to the greatness of God, my very own Heavenly Father.

FORGIVING AND FORGIVEN

What a great story of the power of forgiveness. Not only are we called to receive the Father's forgiveness, we are also called to forgive others even as we have been forgiven. The new robe that we are offered is not only a robe in which we receive forgiveness, it is a robe in which we are called to extend forgiveness. We are called to clothe ourselves with Christ – to put on the Son's clothes (which we never deserved). But we are also called to clothe ourselves with forgiveness.

If you have been hurt by your parents, especially by your father – or a father figure – ask God to give you the power to forgive them. Release them from your bitterness and, in the process, experience your own freedom through forgiveness. Forgiveness really is the golden key. It sets us free from our negative judgments and enables us to know the perfect Father intimately. What could be more liberating than that?

CHAPTER 8

ACCEPTING

Get a ring for his finger . . . (Luke's Gospel 15:22).

One thing I shall always remember about my adoptive father Philip Stibbe is his generosity. He never spoiled me as I grew up, but he did give me gifts.

I recall one occasion when I was about 10 years old. I had discovered the writings of Sir Arthur Conan Doyle in my school library. I had become particularly fascinated by the Sherlock Holmes and Professor Challenger stories. When my dad found this out he was thrilled. He had been an undergraduate at Oxford under C.S. Lewis and loved literature. As soon as he knew that I was developing a passion for the same, he drove over to a big bookshop in Oxford and ordered all of Conan Doyle's writings in hardback books. I can still remember the day he presented them to me as a gift (not on my birthday or at Christmas either). I was completely speechless. I still have them and they are a prized possession.

Another incident stands out for me. My father always used to wear a signet ring with the family crest on it. My older brother Giles received a brand new signet ring on his twenty-first birthday. I had always wondered whether my father would do the same for me. Giles was the natural child of my adoptive parents. I suppose in my insecurity I thought they might give such a gift to him – the natural first-born son – but not to me.

I couldn't have been more wrong. When my twenty-first birthday drew near, my father asked me two questions. Would I also like a signet ring? And would I like the family crest on it or something of my own choosing?

I can remember the delight in my heart. It was as if my father was saying once and for all, 'Have no fear. You're accepted, son.'

Today that ring is a very precious symbol not only of my adoptive father's generosity, but also of the fact that he saw no difference between Giles, his natural son, and me, his adopted child.

A RING UPON HIS FINGER

I imagine the prodigal son felt something similar. When he approached home, smelling of the pigpens, his father ran to him, embraced him and kissed him. He then ordered his servants to do two things: first of all to get the special robe reserved for honoured guests and secondly to fetch the family ring and put it on his finger. When the boy returned, he received two gifts: a robe and a ring. Both of them were undeserved.

As we saw in the last chapter, the robe symbolises the fact that the son is forgiven. It was Dad's way of saying, 'I'm wiping the slate clean. This boy is totally pardoned for what he has done.' The ring symbolised something different, something extra. This ring was the family signet ring. It signified a child's position as a son or a daughter. Not only did it signify position, it signified power or authority. Wearing this ring gave the child the right to give orders in the father's name.

In giving this ring, the father was saying in the strongest possible terms, 'You are restored to your position as my son, with all the rights and the privileges that this entails.' There were no conditions attached to this gift. Rather, the gift was completely undeserved and it was totally, 100 per cent free.

What a picture!

Not only is this dad a forgiving father, he is also a giving father. First he forgives, then he gives. And what he gives communicates a message. It has worth in and of itself, yes. But beyond that, the ring is a sign that signifies something far more precious than any material possession.

It signifies 'acceptance'.

This father in Luke chapter 15 is an accepting father. He accepts his son just as he is and he accepts him back into his family.

The son expected nothing and he got everything.

Not only did he receive a robe, he received a ring. Not only did he get a pardon, he also had his position restored as a child in his father's house. I imagine he was completely overwhelmed by his father's love.

So What?

I believe this is extremely important for our understanding of God. One of the things that I have been trying to say throughout this little book is that God is the Father you've been waiting for. He is the Father who loves us like no earthly father ever could. Throughout, I have been underlining the belief that Jesus, the Master Storyteller, was telling us history-making truths about the character of God in the tale of the prodigal son. While most people have tended to focus on the boy and his sins, Jesus was actually far more interested in the father and his love. The dad is the true focus of the story. The father is the real hero of the tale. And he is a window onto the Father heart of God.

When Jesus tells us that the father gives the boy a ring as well as a robe, I don't think for a moment that this is an insignificant or redundant detail. I don't think this is what the literary critics call a 'reality effect' – a little detail that is inserted simply to make the story sound more realistic. I am convinced that this ring carries as much importance as the robe. While I am aware of the dangers of turning every part of the story into an allegory, I am also sure that Jesus meant something by these details. They are not there by accident.

Many commentators have spent time over the centuries talking about the robe, as I did in the last chapter. Like me, they see significance in the fact that this robe covered the boy's shame. That in turn leads them (and me) to propose that the robe is a symbol of the pardon won for us at the Cross. Thanks to what Jesus has done at Calvary, he gets all our guilt and shame, and we get all his mercy and forgiveness. He gets our filthy rags. We get his robe of righteousness. That's an amazing deal – a truly great exchange.

But if we stop at the robe and neglect the ring, we are going to sell ourselves and others short. Not only did the boy have his sins forgiven, he also had his position restored. The robe said to him, 'You're forgiven.' The ring said to him, 'You're accepted.' We need the ring as well as the robe.

MY STORY

What does all this really mean? Let me tell the story of my spiritual journey at this point.

In 1977, I was far away from God but I was at a school where God was moving powerfully by his Holy Spirit. This school, when I arrived in 1974, was a godless place. There were only five or six Christians out of 450–500 pupils. In many ways the school was suffering from a severe case of intellectual pride. Puffed up by a history of outstanding academic success, pupils did not deem it cool to be a committed Christian. Anyone who decided to be a follower of Jesus was laughed at and regarded as simplistic and dim-witted.

This arrogant attitude prevailed until 1976, when many pupils were touched by God's powerful presence moving through the school. A number of the teenage rebels I hung out with started becoming Christians and having their lives totally transformed. I held out until the last possible minute but in the end surrendered my life to Christ as well.

That happened on the night of 17 January 1977. I was walking down a road called Kingsgate Street when I suddenly felt my heart racing. I had been looking up at the stars in the sky and repeating to myself a line from a Pink Floyd album called 'The Wall'. The line went, 'Is there anybody out there?' As I kept saying this, I sensed a voice in my heart saying 'Yes'. And then a question formed: 'And if you died tonight, where would you stand before the judgment seat of God?'

At that moment I suddenly realised that God is incredibly holy, that we live in a moral universe where all of us are accountable for our actions, and that I myself had lived a self-centred life and didn't have a leg to stand on. As I sensed all this, I knew I needed help. In the language of the Bible, I knew I needed 'saving' or 'rescuing'. Desperate to be pardoned, longing to be sure of going to heaven, I ran round to the house of the teacher who ran the Christian group. Just before midnight, I said a prayer on the floor of his front room and chose to follow Jesus Christ for the rest of my life.

That was a real turning point for me. But it was by no means the end. From that night on I knew that God was a perfect, holy Judge and that I was a sinner. I also knew that thanks to what Jesus did on the Cross I was pardoned. This meant that I no longer wore my own filthy rags but Christ's robe of righteousness. To use the language of the Bible, I was 'justified'. It was 'just-as-if-I'd' never sinned.

But there was more for me to receive. For nearly ten years I knew God as a Judge but not as a Father. I had problems deep down with calling God 'Father' in any case. As I wrote in the introduction, my natural father had walked out on my twin sister and me even before we were born. The word 'father' didn't have very positive connotations in my soul. Knowing God in this intimate way was too painful. So I suppressed that aspect of his character, choosing instead to relate simply to Jesus.

But in 1986 all that changed. I found myself in a conference in Derby with hundreds of other Christians worshipping and praising God. A song struck up with the following words:

Father God, I wonder how I managed to exist
Without the knowledge of your parenthood
And your loving care.
But now I am your child,
I am adopted in your family,
And I shall never be alone
Because Father God
You're there beside me.

As I sang that song for the first time, I suddenly saw that God was not like the dad who abandoned me but like the dad who had adopted me. As I saw that God is my perfect Father – my adoptive, ever-present dad – I fell to my knees. Now I felt complete. Not only was I justified, I was adopted. Not only did I know God as Judge, I also knew him as Father. Not only did I know my pardon, I also knew my position. To put it in the language of the parable of parables, I now had the ring as well as the robe. I now knew I was accepted, not just forgiven.

YOU NEED THE RING AS WELL AS THE ROBE

The sad fact is that many people become Christians but they stop short of receiving the fullness of what the Father has for them. Many Christians I have met over the years have come to the Cross and known God's pardon, but they have never gone one step further to enjoy their new position as sons and daughters. To use some technical language, they have entered into their justification but not their adoption. They know God as Judge but not as Dad.

It is quite amazing how many Christians have stopped short. Even the great Martin Luther, who put justification on the map in the time of the Reformation, had problems knowing God intimately as his Father. His relationship with his own earthly father had been very poor indeed. Consequently, Luther found it really hard relating to God as a father – or better still, as the perfect Father. Consequently, he found it really hard praying as Jesus taught us to pray, to the one we call 'Our Father'. As he himself wrote:

> I have difficulty praying the Lord's Prayer because whenever I say 'Our Father', I think of my own father who was hard, unyielding and relentless. I cannot help but think of God in that way.

I believe the consequences of this have been massive. Martin Luther developed a picture of God as Judge and of Jesus Christ as the one who suffered the penalty we deserved. In talking about our relationship with God, he resorted to the language of the law court. All this is perfectly biblical. There is definitely a legal side to the way the Bible talks about God's plan of rescue or salvation.

But there is also a very relational side. Not only is God the perfect Judge, whose justice is absolutely pure and true, he is also the perfect Father, whose love is absolutely free and enduring. To dwell only on the legal side of God's character is really misleading. We need the relational side too. We need to know we are adopted as well as justified.

The great devotional writer Andrew Murray once put it like this:

The great downfall of the Christian life is that, even where we trust Christ, we leave the Father out. Christ came to bring us to God, the Father. . . . His life of dependency on the Father was a life in the Father's love. . . . Our life must have its breath and being in a heavenly love as much as his. What the Father's love was to him, his love will be to us.

I couldn't agree with that statement more. We need to know God as Father, not just as Judge.

About ten years ago I wrote a book called *From Orphans to Heirs*. The subtitle was 'celebrating your spiritual adoption'. In this book I told the story of how a friend of mine in the United States had adopted his son. He and his wife had gone to a law court where a judge had sat before them. He had read them the requirements for adoption in the strongest possible terms. My friends recalled how nervous they had felt as the judge spoke in such a grave and sombre tone. Then he asked them, 'Do you want me to sign this adoption paper so you can adopt your son?' The couple looked at each other and then said yes.

At that moment the judge walked towards them and placed the paper on the table where my friends were sitting. Before he signed the certificate he looked at them and, with tears in his eyes, said these words: 'This is the best decision you could possibly make. And I know that, because I am a dad who adopted a child. Even though there have been difficult times, I don't regret that decision for a moment.'

You see what happened there? The judge came down and revealed himself as a dad.

That's what many Christians need today. They need to know God as 'Daddy' not just as 'Judge'. They need to come out of the law court and into the living room.

To put it in the language of the parable, they need the ring as well as the robe.

CONVINCED OF YOUR ACCEPTANCE

The year was 1888 and Campbell Morgan was one of 150 young men who sought entrance to ordained ministry in the Wesleyan Church. He passed the doctrinal examinations but then faced the ordeal of preaching a trial sermon. Campbell Morgan found himself in a large auditorium capable of seating one thousand people. The only people there, however, were three examiners and seventy-five others who had come to listen. When Morgan stood to deliver his message, he started looking into the eyes of those ready to critique his every word. He was caught short and delivered the message in a faltering voice. Several weeks later Morgan learned that along with many others he had been rejected for the ministry. His daughter-in-law Jill Morgan later wrote, 'He wired to his father the one word, "Rejected", and sat down to write in his diary: "Very dark everything seems. Still, He knows best." Quickly came the reply: "Rejected on earth. Accepted in heaven. Dad."'

How can we become as convinced, as Campbell Morgan was, that we are 'accepted in heaven'?

I believe the answer to that question lies mainly in the Bible. The Bible is our Father's book. It is his word to the spiritual orphans of this world. It is his message of love to the fatherless.

In this book, or better still, library of books, there are many promises made by God for those who become his children. Those who truly believe these promises become convinced not only of their pardon but also of their position. They become certain not only that they are justified but also that they are adopted. Believing the promises of the Bible is accordingly vital if we are to know our true status as the adopted sons and daughters of God.

A friend of mine called Barry Adams has composed what he calls *Father's Love Letter*. This is a compilation of Bible verses from both the Old and the New Testaments that send the message of God's loving acceptance. Each verse is accompanied by a paraphrase of its message, applied to you and me today.

Barry put this letter together one Sunday morning when he was asked to preach in his church. Since then this letter has been translated into many different languages and read by millions all over the world. It is one of the most powerful resources I have seen for communicating the wonderful truth of the Father's acceptance and affection towards those who turn to him. As Barry says in his introduction:

> The Bible says that God is love. Pure love. And he wants to lavish his love on you. He is not looking for more servants to add to his Kingdom but more children to fill his house. He wants to be in relationship with you, not because you deserve it but just because he made you, and is 'head over heels' in love with you. It is our hope that after reading this letter, you might have a better understanding of his heart for you.

In conclusion, I would like to encourage you to ask the Holy Spirit right now to reveal the Father's love to you. As you read these words, pray that the Father will not only put his robe of righteousness around your shoulders but also his ring of acceptance on your finger. You need the ring as well as the robe. May the words you are about to read go very deep into your soul.

My child . . .

You may not know me, but I know everything about you
. . . Psalm 139:1

I know when you sit down and when you rise up
. . . Psalm 139:2

I am familiar with all your ways
. . . Psalm 139:3

Even the very hairs on your head are numbered
. . . Matthew 10:29–31

For you were made in my image
. . . Genesis 1:27

In me you live and move and have your being
. . . Acts 17:28

For you are my offspring
. . . Acts 17:28

I knew you even before you were conceived
. . . Jeremiah 1:4–5

I chose you when I planned creation
. . . Ephesians 1:11–12

You were not a mistake, for all your days
are written in my book
. . . Psalm 139:15–16

I determined the exact time of your birth
and where you would live
...Acts 17:26

You are fearfully and wonderfully made
...Psalm 139:14

I knit you together in your mother's womb
...Psalm 139:13

And brought you forth on the day you were born
...Psalm 71:6

I have been misrepresented by those who don't know me
...John 8:41–44

I am not distant and angry,
but am the complete expression of love
...1 John 4:16

And it is my desire to lavish my love on you
...1 John 3:1

Simply because you are my child and I am your Father
...1 John 3:1

I offer you more than your earthly father ever could
...Matthew 7:11

For I am the perfect father
...Matthew 5:48

Every good gift that you receive comes from my hand
. . . James 1:17

For I am your provider and I meet all your needs
. . . Matthew 6:31–33

My plan for your future has always been filled with hope
. . . Jeremiah 29:11

Because I love you with an everlasting love
. . . Jeremiah 31:3

My thoughts towards you are countless
as the sand on the seashore
. . . Psalms 139:17–18

And I rejoice over you with singing
. . . Zephaniah 3:17

I will never stop doing good to you
. . . Jeremiah 32:40

For you are my treasured possession
. . . Exodus 19:5

I desire to establish you with all my heart and all my soul
. . . Jeremiah 32:41

And I want to show you great and marvellous things
. . . Jeremiah 33:3

If you seek me with all your heart, you will find me
... Deuteronomy 4:29

Delight in me and I will give you the desires of your heart
... Psalm 37:4

For it is I who gave you those desires
... Philippians 2:13

I am able to do more for you than you could possibly imagine
... Ephesians 3:20

For I am your greatest encourager
... 2 Thessalonians 2:16–17

I am also the Father who comforts you in all your troubles
... 2 Corinthians 1:3–4

When you are broken-hearted, I am close to you
... Psalm 34:18

As a shepherd carries a lamb,
I have carried you close to my heart
... Isaiah 40:11

One day I will wipe away every tear from your eyes
... Revelation 21:3–4

And I'll take away all the pain
you have suffered on this earth
... Revelation 21:3–4

I am your Father, and I love you even as I love my son, Jesus
. . . John 17:23

For in Jesus, my love for you is revealed
. . . John 17:26

He is the exact representation of my being
. . . Hebrews 1:3

He came to demonstrate that I am for you, not against you
. . . Romans 8:31

And to tell you that I am not counting your sins
. . . 2 Corinthians 5:18–19

Jesus died so that you and I could be reconciled
. . . 2 Corinthians 5:18–19

His death was the ultimate expression of my love for you
. . . 1 John 4:10

I gave up everything I loved that I might gain your love
. . . Romans 8:31–32

If you receive the gift of my son Jesus, you receive me
. . . 1 John 2:23

And nothing will ever separate you from my love again
. . . Romans 8:38–39

*Come home and I'll throw the biggest party
heaven has ever seen*
. . . Luke 15:7

I have always been Father, and will always be Father
. . . Ephesians 3:14–15

My question is . . . Will you be my child?
. . . John 1:12–13

I am waiting for you
. : . Luke 15:11–32

Love, your Dad. Almighty God.

CHAPTER 9

EXTRAVAGANT

And sandals for his feet . . . (Luke's Gospel 15:22).

Recently, two friends of ours contacted us from Kyrgyzstan. They sent the following report of a miracle that God had performed in an orphanage, and with socks:

A missionary colleague of ours who is involved in an orphanage here was going to visit the 120 orphans, as she usually does a few times a week. This day was different however, as on her last visit she had noticed that the children of all ages didn't have any socks on and the weather was not very warm either. Normally, the children are somewhat overdressed at the first signs of autumn. So when our friend asked the staff why the children didn't have any socks, she said they'd worn them out and didn't have any, nor did the orphanage have any money to buy socks for so many children.

Our friend gathered up all the socks she could get hold of, and as she was going to the orphanage she discovered that she only had eighty pairs of socks. She realised that she couldn't give them to only some children and leave out the other forty children, so she decided not to say anything.

When she arrived at the orphanage, however, one of the staff said to her, 'Have you brought the socks today?' She couldn't lie and say 'No', so she said, 'Yes, I've brought them with me.' She was about to say that she didn't have enough when the lady said to her, 'The children are all sitting down to eat; why don't you give them out?' So our friend started to give each child a pair of socks very reluctantly.

The amazing thing is that she ended up giving every child a pair of socks and then had twenty-five pairs left over. She had enough for eighty children, but another sixty-five pairs miraculously appeared from nowhere. As when Jesus multiplied the bread, once again there was something left over. This is a great example of the extravagant generosity of God!

A NEW PAIR OF SHOES

In the story of the prodigal son we have reached the point where the father has embraced and kissed his child, and given him a robe and a ring. Now Jesus reports that the dad attended to the needs of his feet.

We need to remember at this point that the boy had lost absolutely everything in the distant country. This would have included his footwear. In all likelihood he had returned wearing nothing on his feet. In the culture of his day, only slaves went about barefoot. The clear implication is that the son had been living as a slave. He had become a slave to money, certainly. His excessive dependency on material wealth had led to him hitting rock-bottom. Prostitution had led to destitution. When he returns to his father's house he arrives as a slave, not as a son.

But his father doesn't let him stay like that. He covers him with a robe and puts a ring on his finger. Now he orders the servants to fetch some shoes and put them on his feet.

There are two words for 'shoe' in Greek. The first word is *sandalon*, from which get 'sandal'. This was a simple shoe that the poor would wear.

The second word is *hupodema*. This was a smart shoe made of leather, and worn by the better-off. These shoes were luxury items, not basic sandals.

When the father asks for shoes, he asks for the second kind, not the first. He asks for shoes befitting an honoured son, not the shoes worn by a servant.

So even though the boy has come back as a slave, he is given the shoes worn by the free. The boy had chosen a life of slavery and had come back ready to negotiate being a servant. But the father's actions are a declaration that he doesn't want his boy to live as a slave or a servant but as a son.

This father is accordingly an extravagant father. He is lavish in his love. He is liberal in his generosity.

Not only does the boy get a robe and a ring, he also gets a quality pair of shoes.

His dad needn't have done that, but he did!

WHO IS TRULY 'PRODIGAL' HERE?

All this makes me wonder why on earth people keep calling this story the parable of the prodigal son. Jesus never gave this title to the story, nor was it put in the original manuscripts of the Gospel of Luke. It has been added over the course of time to our English translations, along with chapter and verse numbers (which are not in the original scripts either).

There are two reasons why I think it is wrong to call this story the parable of the prodigal son.

First, as I have frequently commented throughout this book, the son is not the focus of the story, the father is. He is the one who takes centre stage throughout the narrative. We should have got the hint from the opening sentence. 'There was a man who had two sons'... i.e. a *father*! Not, 'There was a son who went off the rails.' Jesus points right at the start of the story to the one he regards as central.

Secondly, the son could be said to be 'prodigal', by all means. He was extravagantly wasteful with his father's money. But the word 'prodigal' can be applied to one other figure in the story, to the father.

The word 'prodigal' is defined in the Collins English Dictionary as 'extravagant, recklessly wasteful, generous in giving', from the Latin *prodigus*, meaning 'lavish'. Now we automatically think of this word in a negative sense, as extravagant in the wrong way. But there is no reason why this word could not be used in a positive way, meaning extravagant in relation to good things.

If that is true, the word can be used of the father and we can rename the story The Parable of the Prodigal Father. He is the one who is extravagant and lavish – not with money and possessions, as the younger son is, but with patience and love.

For a long time I have been proposing that this story be renamed the Parable of the Prodigal Father. It is truly the Father's story, both in the sense that it tells the story of an amazing dad, and in the bigger sense that it tells the story of the one whom Jesus taught us to address as 'Our Father'. Both dads are prodigious in their loving!

SO WHAT?

It's incredibly important that we place the focus where it was always intended to be in the parable of parables. While we keep the spotlight on the wayward son, we are always likely to compare ourselves with him and run the risk of morbid introspection. But if we allow the spotlight to fall upon the father, we are more likely to compare him with

God the Father, and in the process see some compelling reasons for wanting to relate to him as loving sons and daughters.

For he is truly worth knowing.

Like the prodigal, extravagantly loving father in the story, God the Father has lavished his love upon the world. In John's Gospel (chapter 3, verse 16) we learn:

For God so loved the world that he gave his only Son, so that everyone who believes in him will not perish but have eternal life.

John's Gospel also shows us that Jesus, God's Son, came to tell us what our Heavenly Father is really like. In chapter 1, verse 18, we hear that

No one has ever seen God. But his only Son, who is himself God, is near to the Father's heart; he has told us about him.

Those who accept Jesus Christ and choose to believe in him get to become God's adopted children and to know God as their perfect Dad (John 1:12–13):

To all who believed him and accepted him, he gave the right to become children of God. They are reborn!

To everyone who chooses to follow and love the Son, the following words apply (John 16:27):

The Father himself loves you dearly because you love me and believe that I came from God.

THE LAVISH LOVE OF GOD

The key to understanding the New Testament is simply this: if you want to get to know the Father you have to get to know the Son. The Son introduces us to the Father, no one else does, and the Father has gone to extraordinary lengths to adopt us as his children. In Jesus Christ, God has loved us to death. He has literally gone to hell and back to demonstrate how high, how deep, how long and how wide is his love for you and me. This is extravagant, prodigal love indeed. As Saint John puts it, this time in his first letter (chapter 3, verse 1, NIV):

How great is the love the Father has lavished on us, that we should be called children of God! And that is what we are!

Saint Paul makes a similar point at the start of his letter to the Ephesians. He starts off this letter by giving praise to the Father for all the blessings that we have received from heaven thanks to Jesus Christ. First in the list of blessings is the fact that those who believe in Jesus are adopted as his sons and daughters. In chapter 1, verses 7–8, he goes on to add another blessing:

In him we have redemption through his blood, the forgiveness of sins, in accordance with the riches of God's grace that he lavished on us (NIV).

Thanks to what Jesus did on the Cross, we have been redeemed, we have been bought out of slavery to sin and set free. It was through the blood Jesus shed that this freedom and forgiveness has come our way. And all this happened because of the riches of God's amazing grace. Out of the inestimable wealth of his love, the Father has lavished spiritual blessings upon us. We didn't deserve these. But the Father still gave them, and they are free for all those who choose to believe in his Son.

THE KING'S GENEROSITY

The extravagant love of the father in the parable is accordingly a signpost towards the amazing grace of our Father in heaven. Grace is a word you find a lot in the Bible. When it is applied to God it means his divine favour and affection. The nation of Israel was the first to experience this grace when the Father set his affections upon them and adopted them as his people. He did this not because of any merit on their part but simply because he couldn't help loving them. It was in his nature. His love was unmerited, but it was given.

And the same is true for those who have chosen to put their trust in Jesus Christ as their Lord and Saviour. They too have received the grace of God. They too have received the undeserved favour of the perfect Dad. They have been adopted and chosen to be God's daughters and sons – something that has brought the Father great delight. And this dad doesn't hold back on his gifts. He gives us one blessing after another. He gives us forgiveness for all our past wrongdoing. He gives us new life in the present by granting us special abilities to fulfil our life's mission. And he gives us a hope for the future – a destiny to fulfil, a reason for getting up every day, a real purpose for living. In fact, as the King of kings, God has infinite resources at his disposal when he gives us the riches of his grace. And he gives to his people far more than they ever ask or imagine.

One day a beggar by the roadside asked for money from Alexander the Great as he passed by. The man was poor and wretched and had no claim upon the ruler, no right even to lift a solicitous hand. Yet the Emperor threw him several gold coins. A courtier was astonished at his generosity and commented, 'Sir, copper coins would adequately meet a beggar's need. Why give him gold?' Alexander responded in royal fashion, 'Copper coins would suit the beggar's need, but gold coins suit Alexander's giving.'

God the Father is the King of kings, and gives far more abundantly than we deserve. That's what's so amazing about his grace!

THE STORY OF GEORGE MÜLLER

Not long ago, I had the privilege of speaking about my adoption at Müller House in Bristol. Müller House is the headquarters of a ministry founded by the man who did more for orphans than any other human being in British history. His name was George Müller, and his story is a story of the amazing grace of the perfect Father.

Müller was born in a Prussian village in 1805. He spent his teenage years in complete hedonism. His father was generous to him financially, but Müller spent the large amounts of money given to him and then resorted to lying and stealing to acquire more. He went from one hotel to another, pursuing pleasure and living the playboy life. In the end, he ran out of money after pawning his last possessions. He was eventually arrested and ended up in prison.

When he was 20 years old, Müller came to his senses. He was invited by a friend called Beta to a home where Christians were meeting to pray. Müller agreed and that night, in November 1825, his whole life was changed. He was overwhelmed by the sense of God's love among these sincere Christians. Their welcome warmed him. Their simple, heartfelt prayers to God impressed him deeply. Some time later, George Müller wrote this about that evening meeting:

I understood something of the reason why the Lord Jesus died on the Cross and suffered agonies in the Garden of Gethsemane; even that thus, bearing the punishment due to us, we might not have to bear it ourselves. And therefore, apprehending in some measure the love of Jesus for my soul, I was constrained to love him in return.

George Müller had been like the son in the parable of parables. As many commentators have seen, his life parallels the wayward journey of the younger son in Luke 15 in some remarkable ways. But Müller found his way home. He experienced the amazing grace of God.

Müller's story doesn't end there. In 1832 he came to Bristol. There he was struck by the number of children made homeless by the cholera epidemics. From 1835 on, Müller set up five homes for orphans in Ashley Down, Bristol. They housed more than two thousand children. When Müller died in 1898, seven thousand people crowded the streets for his funeral. One of them, an orphan who had benefited from Müller's ministry, said, 'The greatest thing that has ever happened to me was at the Müller Homes because there I learnt about the Lord Jesus. Through the teaching that had been put in my heart as a child, I gave that same heart to the Lord one day, and have never regretted it.'

All this is remarkable enough. But the most amazing thing of all was Müller's attitude towards money and material things. Müller never once made a charitable appeal. He simply prayed for his Father to release funds and food to the orphans, trusting in the promises of God in the Bible with childlike faith. During those decades in Bristol, people gave the equivalent of £75 million to this ministry. Others gave food and clothes, and always in response to Müller's prayers, not to direct appeals.

Take, for example, the day when at breakfast-time there was no food. Müller took the hand of a small girl and said, 'Come and see what the Father will do.' There was no food and no money, but Müller prayed, 'Dear Father, we thank you for what you are going to give us to eat.' Immediately, they heard a knock at the door and found a local baker standing there. 'Mr Müller,' he said, 'I couldn't sleep last night. Somehow I felt you had no bread for breakfast, so I got up at 2 o'clock and baked fresh bread. Here it is.' Müller thanked him and gave praise to God. Soon, a second knock was heard. It was the milkman. His cart had broken down in front of the orphanage. He said he would like to give the children the milk so he could empty the cart and repair it.

Müller's life is an extraordinary example of how one man received the extravagant and lavish love of the Father, and then gave that same love away to the fatherless. Psalm 68:5 says, 'Father to the fatherless, defender of widows – this is

God, whose dwelling is holy.' Müller's life was a reflection of
the perfect Father.

CHILDLIKE FAITH BEFORE GOD

If George Müller were alive today, he would say that the key
to receiving the abundant generosity of God is simple faith.
Müller relied on faith from the moment of his conversion
onwards. When he submitted his life to Jesus, he chose to
believe in someone he couldn't see with his physical eyes.
Christians believe that Jesus is alive because he has risen from
the dead. But we cannot see him. Jesus said, 'Blessed are those
who haven't seen me and believe anyway' (John 20:29).

From his conversion onwards, George Müller believed
on the basis of what the Bible says rather than what he saw
with his eyes. Often, as in the breakfast incident described
above, there was no evidence of the object of his praying. In
a time of great need, Müller did not rely on his physical
senses or look at the outward circumstances. Instead, he put
his trust in the Word of God and the goodness of God.
Müller's life was the life of simple faith – the faith of a child
before its Father. As Müller used to say, 'Ask the Lord, in
childlike simplicity.'

This means that the key to becoming filled is becoming
empty. The key to becoming rich spiritually is becoming
poor in spirit. As Müller said:

Faith does not operate in the realm of the possible. There is no glory for God in that which is humanly possible. Faith begins where man's power ends.

When we are desperate, that is the time when faith can kick in. All our sophisticated thinking, our self-reliance, our material strength is gone. We have nothing. In this place of weakness, we start believing, as Müller did, that the Father's power can do far more than we could ever ask or imagine. Or, in Müller's own words, that the King of kings 'can give us more than we need'. In our spiritual and material poverty, the Father's lavish love is accessed by simple faith. The gap between earthly want and heaven's resources is bridged through childlike prayer. Faith unlocks the riches of his grace.

So have faith. Believe in the one you cannot see. Believe for the things that are not yet visible. If you are a Christian, your Father is the King of kings. Your Saviour, Jesus, is the Prince of Peace. In heaven, there is no shortage of resources. If you are walking in the will of God, believe that God can do *extravagantly* more than you realise. The father gave his son far more than he deserved or needed in Luke 15. Our Heavenly Father does the same for us today.

The following story illustrates the point.

The golfer Arnold Palmer was once invited by a Saudi prince to play golf with him. The prince sent his private jet to pick Arnold up and they had a wonderful time playing golf together.

When it was time for Palmer to go home, the prince wanted to give him a gift, as a token of appreciation for his visit. Arnold at first demurred, but finally consented, and told the prince that he collected golf clubs and would appreciate a new club for his collection.

Upon returning home, the golfer checked his mailbox on a daily basis, waiting for what he was sure would be an exquisite club – perhaps gold, maybe encrusted with jewels – but the mailbox was empty.

Finally, he found an envelope from the prince. Confused as to how a golf club could be contained in an envelope, he opened the letter.

Inside was the deed to an American golf 'club'.

Never forget: when it comes to gift giving, princes and kings think differently from ordinary people like you and me.

In whatever kind of poverty you find yourself, believe that your royal Father can give you more than you could ever ask or imagine.

And pray, like George Müller, with simple, childlike faith in the Father.

CHAPTER 10

REJOICING

'And kill the calf we have been fattening in the pen. We must celebrate with a feast, for this son of mine was dead and has now returned to life. He was lost, but now he is found.' So the party began (Luke's Gospel 15:23–24).

O ne of the most challenging stories I have heard concerns sociologist Tony Campolo. A few years ago, Tony flew from the United States mainland to Honolulu. Because of the jet lag he woke at 3 o'clock in the morning with his body thinking it was 9 o'clock and time for breakfast. He got up, and wandered down the street from the hotel into a restaurant – a rather grotty, dirty place. He ordered a cup of coffee and a doughnut.

The man behind the counter was an unkempt man named Harry. Harry handed Tony a doughnut. While he was drinking and eating, the door burst open and eight or nine boisterous prostitutes came in. They sat down at the counter next to Tony.

One of the women said, 'Tomorrow is my birthday. I'll be 39.' Her friend said, 'So what do you want from me? I suppose you want a party or something. Maybe you want me to bake you a cake.'

The first woman (whom he later found out was named Agnes) said, 'Why are you so mean? I don't want anything from you. I've never had a birthday party and no one has ever baked me a cake. Be quiet!'

At that point Tony got an idea. When the ladies had left he said to Harry behind the counter, 'Do they come in here every night?'

'Yes, they do.'

'This one next to me – Agnes?'

'Same time, just like clockwork.'

So Tony said, 'What about if we throw a party for her, a birthday party?'

Harry began to smile and called to his wife and they agreed it was a wonderful idea and they made plans.

The next night Tony came back at the same time and the place was decorated with crepe paper and a sign on the wall which said, 'Happy Birthday, Agnes.' It had been cleaned up and looked like a different place. They sat down and waited. Soon others began to trickle in. Word had got round on the streets and prostitutes from all over Honolulu arrived.

At the regular time, Agnes and her friends burst through the door and everyone shouted, 'Happy birthday, Agnes!' Her knees buckled. Her friends caught her. She was stunned. They led her to the counter and she sat down. Harry brought the cake out and her mouth fell open and her eyes filled with tears. They put the cake down in front of her and sang 'Happy Birthday'.

Harry said, 'Blow the candles out so we can all have some.' But Agnes just stared at the cake. Finally they convinced her to blow out the candles. Harry handed her a knife and told her to cut the cake. She sat looking at the cake lovingly as if it was the most precious thing she had ever seen. Then she said, 'Do I have to cut it?'

Harry said, 'Well, no, I suppose you don't have to cut it.'

Then she said something even more strange: 'I would like to keep it for a while. I don't live far from here. Can I take it home? I'll be right back.'

Everybody looked at her with puzzled faces and said, 'Sure, you can take it.'

She picked up the cake and carried it, as if she was carrying the Holy Grail, and walked out the door.

There was stunned silence. Then Tony Campolo started sharing with those left behind about Jesus. Harry said to him, 'Hey, I didn't know you were a preacher.'

Tony answered, 'I'm not a preacher. I'm a sociologist.'

Harry asked, 'Well, what kinda church do you come from anyway?'

Tony, inspired by God's Spirit, said, 'I guess I come from a church that throws birthday parties for prostitutes at 3 o'clock in the morning.'

And Harry said, 'No you don't. There's no such church like that, 'cause if there was, I'd join it.'

KILLING THE FATTED CALF

The parable of parables ends with a great party. Not only did the son receive a robe, a ring and a pair of shoes; he also received the 'fatted calf'. The father was not only a forgiving father; he was truly a giving dad too.

The fatted calf was a grain-fed animal reserved for celebrating the presence of honoured guests and visiting dignitaries. A beast like this would easily feed between one and two hundred people. It is perhaps worth adding that the whole animal would have been eaten in a short space of time, otherwise it would have gone off. Clearly, a great number of people were invited to this party.

When the father declared 'we must celebrate', he was not just referring to his own household – including the older brother and the hired servants. He was referring to the whole village. In effect, the father was throwing a party for all those who had gossiped about and even slandered the boy who had left home in such disgrace. This shows that the father wanted to make his forgiveness public. He wanted everyone to honour the reconciliation that he had orchestrated.

So this dad threw a party for the whole community. The reason he gives is simple:

We must celebrate with a feast, for this son of mine was dead and has now returned to life. He was lost, but now he is found (Luke 15:23–24).

This piece of news goes round all the neighbours. The arrangements are made without delay, and Jesus simply adds the words, 'So the party began.'

The parable had begun with a great rejection. It now comes to a conclusion with a great reconciliation. It had begun with great sorrow, but now it concludes with great rejoicing. It had begun with the boy giving himself over to death, but now it ends with him returning to life. It had begun with the son being lost, but now it ends with the son being found. All this calls for a party.

A TALE OF TWO PARTIES

The party this dad threw for his son was a great banquet with music and dancing. This means tambourines, drums, and plucked instruments (like today's guitars). It was a joyful celebration. But Luke's Gospel also tells us about a different kind of party. In Luke chapter 12, verse 19, we read of a rich man who became even richer and decided to build bigger and bigger barns to store his newly accumulated resources.

With no care at all for his soul, he said to himself, 'Now take it easy! Eat, drink and be merry!' The Greek word translated here 'be merry' is the same as the one used to describe the father's celebration in the parable of parables. Only this time the word refers to self-indulgent partying – the kind based on hedonism and living purely for the moment.

It is important to understand that there are two kinds of party in this parable. The first was the kind of party that the boy wanted when he left home. This kind of partying is self-focused. It is like the partying of the rich man in Luke 12:19, or the feasting of the wealthy man called Dives in Luke 16:19. This kind of party is shallow, empty, fleeting and wasteful.

In contrast to all this is the father's party. It has many of the same ingredients – great food, great music, great dancing. But it is different from the partying the son had experienced earlier. The biggest difference is the reason for the party. In the earlier part of the parable the reason for the son's partying was idolatry. It was focused on the worship of self. At the end of the story, the father's party is focused on something quite different. It is focused on the father's loving welcome that he gives his boy on his return from the far country. The first kind of party was held for the pursuit of pleasure. The second was held to celebrate a miracle.

Welcoming the Lost

It's really important at this point to remember Luke chapter 15 as a whole, not just the part of the chapter that includes the parable of the loving father. In fact, Jesus tells two other stories before he tells this one. He tells the story of a shepherd who has one hundred sheep but loses one. He leaves the ninety-nine behind in search of the one lost. He finds the lost sheep and then holds a party to celebrate. Jesus concludes:

> *In the same way, heaven will be happier over one lost sinner who returns to God than over ninety-nine others who are righteous and haven't strayed away!*

There's the party theme again!

Jesus then tells the story of a woman who has ten coins but loses one. She searches the whole of her house until she locates the lost coin. When she has found it, she calls her neighbours in and holds a party. Jesus concludes:

> *In the same way, there is joy in the presence of God's angels when even one sinner repents.*

There's the party theme again!

Why does Jesus emphasise feasting and merry-making in Luke 15? The answer can be found in the first two verses, where we learn to whom these three parables (the lost sheep, the lost coin and the lost son) were addressed. Luke reports that:

Tax collectors and other notorious sinners often came to listen to Jesus teach. This made the Pharisees and teachers of religious law complain that he was associating with such despicable people – even eating with them!

The parables were addressed to 'religious people'.

What kind of 'religious people' were these? This is not the place to look at 'Pharisees' and 'teachers of religious law'. The one important thing to note about the representatives of these groups is simply this: they could not stand the fact that Jesus loved eating and drinking with tax collectors and notorious sinners. To put it another way, they could not tolerate the inclusive nature of Jesus' welcome. They did not understand that the Kingdom Jesus came to introduce was an 'open set', where prostitutes were welcome and the worst lawbreakers could receive the Father's love. They wanted Jesus to promote a 'closed set' with fixed and firm boundaries. With their very dogmatic ideas of 'clean' and 'unclean', of who's in and who's out, they had no room for this kind of alternative society. They did not want a community in which sinners could find the extravagant compassion of God.

So Jesus tells these three parables to challenge his listeners, and every listener like them in future generations. Jesus of Nazareth came not only to comfort the afflicted but also to afflict the comfortable. And he particularly afflicted the religious hypocrites of his day who claimed to be the real thing but were the farthest from that. In fact, Jesus reserved his harshest critiques for the judgmental, religious hypocrites who were not prepared to join in with the joyful and inclusive welcome of the Kingdom of God.

And that, finally, is why the older brother appears in the parable. No sooner has the lost son come home and had a party started in his honour than his older brother begins to moan. He has been working in the fields when he hears the commotion and the celebration beginning. Jesus says that when he finds out from the servants what's going on he is 'angry' and won't come in to the party, because his brother has squandered his money on prostitutes. The father comes out and begs his older son to come in, but the story ends without an answer. In fact, we never know how the older son reacts. The ending is open. It is as if Jesus was saying to the religious people then, and to every reader today, 'You write the ending of the story.' And in writing it, we decide our destiny.

So What?

This book has been about our image or picture of God. I have proposed that Jesus told the parable of parables in order to paint a picture of what his Father in heaven is really like. In the parable, the dad is the real focus of the story and the hero of the tale. He proves to be patient, waiting, compassionate, running, affectionate, intimate, forgiving, accepting, extravagant and rejoicing. Not only are these ten characteristics true of the fictional dad in the story, they are also true of our living Father in heaven. The God revealed by Jesus is the Father you've been waiting for. He is the Father who loves us like no earthly father ever could.

And the last of these ten great qualities is worth emphasising for a moment. I wonder whether you've ever thought of God as one who rejoices. I wonder whether you've ever seen God as a party-throwing Dad. In Chapter 3 we saw how God is sometimes a weeping Father. But here, in this final chapter, we see he can also be a laughing Father – a Father who is passionate about partying and able to rejoice with great abandonment. I wonder whether you've ever imagined God like that.

I remember speaking at a conference in Norway. I took a team of people from my church. It was winter and the place we went to was covered in a brilliant carpet of thick snow. To my team and me this was all too much. As soon as we got out of the minibus at the church, we spent at least an hour throwing snowballs at each other and having a great laugh. In fact, for the next three days of the conference, we couldn't stop laughing.

When the conference came to an end, the host stood in front of the crowd to thank us. He made what to us was a most revealing statement. He thanked us for all that we had taught and ministered, but he thanked us most of all for our laughter. He pointed out that in Norway, 'Joy is a very serious thing' (people laughed at this point). He also pointed out that in the church in Norway, religion is put in one box and fun in another. The thing they had learned from us was that you could have religion and fun in the same box.

The parable tells us something immensely important about God: that he is a Dad who smiles and laughs, rejoices and celebrates. God loves a great party. Our Father in heaven is not a cold, miserable Dad. He is a Father who weeps with joy when his children come home.

Looking at the Bible as a whole, we see that the Father loves to rejoice over his children. The oldest blessing in the world is in the Book of Numbers in the Old Testament. At least three thousand years old, the words – found in chapter 6, verses 24–26 – go as follows:

May the LORD bless you and protect you.
May the LORD smile on you and be gracious to you.
May the LORD show you his favour and give you his peace.

Notice the word 'smile'. The Father wants to smile upon his children and wants them to bathe in the warmth of his divine affection.

Then, in the book of the Old Testament prophet Zephaniah, these words are found in chapter 3, verse 17:

The LORD your God has arrived to live among you. He is a mighty saviour. He will rejoice over you with great gladness. With his love, he will calm all your fears. He will exult over you by singing a happy song.

What a wonderful promise to God's people! Here the picture is of the Father going beyond just smiling to rejoicing over us, even singing a happy song.

Passages such as these deal the final deathblow to drab religion, to the morbid and unremitting tedium of so much religious respectability. Going back to the parable in Luke 15, the laughter of the father and the fun of the festival are clear signs that God loves to rejoice, and to rejoice in style. The lesson of all this is that the God revealed by Jesus is not a remote Lawgiver but a relational, rejoicing Father.

REJOICING IN THE HOUSE OF GOD

In 1998, pop artist Boy George wrote an account of his experience of a church service. His account was published in a national daily newspaper:

Churches are glorious places, but don't you wish they were a little more inviting?

On Sunday I attended the christening of my year-old godson Michael and he was as restless as everyone else.

The grown-ups were content to squirm inwardly and eye their watches. Michael was much more honest and aired his discomfort with a holler.

The sermon was based on the Holy Trinity as it was Trinity Sunday, but because I never go to church it was like explaining Shakespeare to a groundhog.

The priest was a lovely man with impeccable dress sense but I was confused from the moment he took the pulpit. Most of us only ever go to church for weddings and funerals, so sticking to the book is pointless.

Only a religious train-spotter would know the stories by heart and what is the point of rattling on about sin when most of us are doomed to eternal damnation? It doesn't warm people to Christianity; it only makes them feel like hypocrites.

Worse still are the utterly depressing hymns. I'd like to see live music, acoustic guitars and percussion. An old Fairy Liquid bottle with dried peas would do just fine.

Church should be a joyous and liberating experience. Little Michael should have been carried in on a fresh-fruit platter and we should have sung, 'He's got the whole world in his hands' or 'Michael, row the boat ashore'.

The church badly needs a facelift because it is God's
theatre on earth and he should be packing them in.

It is hard to argue with these comments. The trouble with
many churches is that they have tended to be unwelcoming,
boring, condemning, musically out of date and visually
colourless. The public perception of church matches Boy
George's experience. The church worships in black and
white rather than glorious technicolour.

But this is exactly the opposite of what the Father has
always wanted. I believe the parable of the loving father in
Luke 15 reveals quite a different picture. In it, we see a father
who loves to celebrate and rejoice. We see a father who
enjoys the sound of guitars and drums and who encourages
his guests to dance. We see a father who has his arms opened
wide towards the lost. We see a father who transmits in his
actions (not in words) a message of loving acceptance of
even the most wayward son and daughter. We see a father
who gives gifts to those who don't deserve it and know they
don't deserve it. That's some father!

And Jesus was saying, 'This is what God the Father is
like!' It's not that he doesn't feel the wounds of our rejection
or neglect. It's not that he doesn't treat sin seriously or that
he isn't holy. It's just that he knows that the best way to woo
us home is with a great display of compassion and grace,
not with thunderous roars of holy wrath. So his longing has

always been for the church to be a joyful place, full of adopted sons and daughters who know the Father's love because they have been welcomed home and forgiven much. His plan has been for the church to be a happy community, full of great music and uninhibited celebration. His desire has always been for his house to be a place of feasting more than fasting. His plan has been for the church to be like the father's house in Luke 15, a place filled with the sound of laughter and songs of joy.

God's invitation is to join his family – a community where there is passionate, inspirational celebration. Thank God there are more and more churches like this today. There are more and more churches obeying the call in Psalm 150, verses 3–6:

> *Praise him with a blast of the trumpet;*
> *praise him with the lyre and harp!*
> *Praise him with the tambourine and dancing;*
> *praise him with stringed instruments and flutes!*
> *Praise him with a clash of cymbals;*
> *praise him with loud clanging cymbals.*
> *Let everything that lives sing praises to the LORD!*

ON EARTH AS IT IS IN HEAVEN

And the reason why all this is important is that the Father wants his church to be a foretaste of heaven, not a trailer for hell. Did you notice what Jesus said at the end of the parables of the lost sheep and the lost coin? He talked about heaven being happy when a lost soul comes home. He talked about the angels rejoicing when just one person in the world returns to his arms of love here on the earth. There are parties in heaven all the time.

When history comes to a conclusion, Jesus will return and lead those who have put their trust in him to his Father's house. As he promised his disciples in John's Gospel chapter 14, verses 1–3,

> *Don't be troubled. You trust God, now trust in me. There are many rooms in my Father's home, and I am going to prepare a place for you. If this were not so, I would tell you plainly. When everything is ready, I will come and get you, so that you will always be with me where I am.*

The truth is that there is going to be the party of all parties in the Father's house at the very end of time. Everyone is invited to this party. But to enter, you need to be wearing the robe of God's forgiveness and the ring of his acceptance. I will describe how you might do that in the conclusion of this book.

I don't know about you, but I think the father in the parable Jesus told in Luke 15 is the best dad you could possibly imagine. If God's really like that, I want to get to know him. I want to establish a relationship with him. I don't want to miss out on heaven's party. I don't want to find there is no room for me in the Father's house. Maybe it's time for you to come home, to the Father you've been waiting for.

CONCLUSION

IT's TIME TO COME HOME

O ne of director Tom Shadyac's more thought-provoking movies is *Patch Adams* (1998). It tells the true story of Hunter 'Patch' Adams, a heroic man who is determined to become a doctor because he loves helping people.

The movie begins with Hunter admitting himself as a patient in a psychiatric hospital. Here he discovers he has a gift for making people laugh and he comes to see the healing power of laughter. He then sets up his own clinic but falls foul of the medical authorities for practising medicine without a proper licence.

This is a marvellous movie that illustrates the truth of a verse in the Bible, in the Book of Proverbs (chapter 17, verse 22), that 'a cheerful heart is good medicine'. But the reason I mention it here is because the movie starts with Patch Adams on a bus going through some spectacular snowy scenery. As the bus nears its destination, we overhear Patch Adams' thoughts. What he says is all about homecoming:

All of life is a coming home. Salesmen, secretaries, coal miners, beekeepers, sword-swallowers – all of us, all the restless hearts of the world, all trying to find a way home.

It's hard to describe what I felt like then. Picture yourself walking for days in a driving snow. You don't even know you're walking in circles. The heaviness of your legs in the drifts, your shouts disappearing into the wind – how small you can feel, how far away from home you can be. 'Home' – the dictionary defines it as both 'a place of origin' and 'a goal, or destination'. And the storm? The storm was all in my mind. Or, as the poet Dante put it, 'In the middle of the journey of my life, I found myself in a dark wood, for I had lost the right path.' Eventually I would find the right path, but in the most unlikely place.

FOUR KEYS TO COMING HOME

This book has been about the Father you've been waiting for. What I've tried to show is that the father in the parable of parables is the most amazing father you could possibly ever imagine. The good news of the parable is this: that the imaginary father is a mirror image of a very real Father – the Father Jesus came to reveal. My conviction is that the goal of our spiritual search, the destination of our religious quest, is in the arms of this Father. True homecoming occurs when we find our way into his divine embrace.

So how do we do that?

The answer lies in the behaviour of the younger son in the story. As we look at what he did, we see four keys to coming home.

KEY NO. 1:
PRAY FOR A SPIRITUAL AWAKENING

In verse 17 of the parable, Jesus said that the boy 'came to his senses'. In the far-off country, having hit rock-bottom, the boy experiences an awakening. Having lived only for the moment, he now looks back and sees what he's missing in terms of his father's love. He compares his current employer with the father of his past. The employer had given him the classic cultural brush-off line, 'If you want a job, you can feed my pigs.' His father had always given him everything he needed. He compares his current diet with his past one. In making these contrasts, the boy begins to realise what he's missing. He has a spiritual awakening.

Maybe your focus is on what Aldous Huxley called getting 'no leisure from pleasure'. Maybe you have forgotten where you have come from and are ignoring where you're going. If you are like the younger son in the story, pray for a spiritual awakening. Pray that you too would come to see your situation as it really is. The younger son found a proper perspective in the pigpen. He recognised that 'at home even the hired men have food enough to spare, and here I am, dying of hunger!' Why live as a slave when you can live as a son or a daughter?

KEY NO. 2:
TURN BACK TOWARDS THE FATHER

The next thing the younger son does is say to himself, 'I will go home to my father.'

Key to all of this is the idea of 'turning around'. One moment he is heading away from his father, the next moment he experiences a U-turn and heads back towards him.

The Bible calls this 'repentance'. Repentance means many things, but at its root it means a change of direction. When we repent we make a conscious decision to change from one way of life to another, from one way of behaving to another. In this, you and I have an active part to play. Repentance doesn't simply happen to us by osmosis. We choose to see things differently, we choose to feel differently about something, we choose to act in a different way from before.

Why am I stressing the active part that you and I have to play? It is because this parable occurs in a chapter where there are two other parables, as I've already shown.

The first parable tells the story of a shepherd who has one hundred sheep. He leaves the ninety-nine and goes off in search of one that's lost.

The second story tells of a lady who has ten coins. She loses one and turns the whole house upside down until she has found the one missing.

The third story tells of a father whose younger son rejects him, leaves home and loses everything in a faraway country. The father waits patiently and lovingly until his boy decides to come back.

I believe one of the main reasons why Jesus told a third story about the son is simply because the sheep and the coin played no part in returning to their shepherd and owner. Sheep and coins, in other words, can't repent. But lost sons and lost daughters can. We can choose to turn around. We can play an active part in changing direction and living near to the Father rather than far away.

C.S. Lewis once said that repentance is simply a description of what going back home is really like. Maybe it's time to make a U-turn back to the Father.

KEY No. 3:
UNDERSTAND WHAT SIN REALLY IS

As the younger son resolves to return to his dad, he acknowledges that he has sinned. This is what he says: 'Father, I have sinned against both heaven and you, and I am no longer worthy of being called your son. Please take me on as a hired man.'

Sin is a word that's out of fashion today. There are many reasons for this, but one of the most important is that we have misunderstood what it means. Many religious people have painted a picture of God as a Lawgiver, and sin as a breaking of these laws. While I can understand this, the truth is that God is a Loving Father much more than he is a Lawgiver.

In the parable of parables it is very important to understand that lawbreaking is not the real issue in the story. There are no laws in the Old Testament forbidding someone from asking for their inheritance while their father is still alive. This means the boy didn't break religious rules when he said, 'I want my inheritance right now.' What he broke was his father's heart.

This, in essence, is what sin really is. Sin is not so much the breaking of God's rules as the breaking of God's heart. God is the most perfect of all dads. When the boy comes home he sees this. His dad runs to him, embraces him, kisses him, and puts a robe on his shoulders, a ring on his finger and shoes on his feet. Confronted by this amazing love, the boy never gets round to saying, 'Take me on as a hired man' as he had intended. He is simply overwhelmed and can only say, 'Dad, I sinned.' As Kenneth Bailey puts it:

Faced with this incredible event that he could never have predicted, he is flooded with the awareness that his real sin is not the lost money but rather the wounding of his father's heart. The reality and enormity of his sin and the resulting intensity of his father's suffering overwhelm him. There is nothing he can do to make up for this. His proposed offer to work as a servant now seems blasphemous.

Understand what sin really is – it's hurting God.

KEY NO. 4:
ENTER INTO THE FATHER'S LOVE

The boy could have rejected his father's love even then. He could have shied away from his dad's embrace. He could have refused the father's gifts. He could have said no to the invitation to the banquet.

The poet Rudyard Kipling wrote his own version of the parable, called simply 'The Prodigal Son'. In it he imagines the boy coming home, being confronted by his father's love, receiving his invitation to the party, but saying no. He imagines the boy choosing to reject this offer, deciding instead to return to the far country to live with the pigs again. This is how Kipling puts it:

Here come I to my own again,
Fed, forgiven and known again,
Claimed by bone of my bone again
And cheered by flesh of my flesh.
The fatted calf is dressed for me,

But the husks have greater zest for me,
I think my pigs will be best for me,
So I'm off to the Yards afresh.

Don't be like Kipling's prodigal. Accept the Father's loving embrace. Accept the Father's invitation to live again. Find a church family where the Father's welcoming love is truly offered. And resolve to stay in relationship to the perfect Father for the rest of your life.

If you would like to do that now, here is a prayer – written by Barry Adams – that you can use to accept or reaffirm your relationship with the Father:

Father, I'm coming home. Please make me your child. I turn from my sin. I accept your forgiveness made possible through Jesus Christ by his death and resurrection. I place my faith and trust in Jesus alone. I receive him as my Saviour and Lord. I want to follow and serve you. Let today be the beginning of my new journey as your child and a member of your family. Thank you for making a way for me to come home. In Jesus' name I pray. Amen.

A STORY OF AMAZING GRACE

One of the best loved hymns of all is John Newton's 'Amazing Grace'. John Newton was brought up by a very devout mother who prayed that one day he would become a minister. She taught him to read the Bible and to recite hymns. When he was 6 years old, John's mother died. His father remarried and John was sent away to boarding school.

When he was 11, his father took him to sea and he spent six years travelling over the oceans. His father was a good man who gave him many opportunities. But John rebelled and squandered all his father's gifts. John strayed as far from his mother's teaching as it's possible to imagine. His life degenerated. He ran from his father's support. He disobeyed his superior officers. He was disliked and distrusted by the crews he sailed with. He was so godless he was known as 'the Great Blasphemer'.

John changed ships and joined a slave trader from West Africa. The slave trader's wife was an African princess who greatly disliked John. When her husband was away, she abused John by having him locked up in chains as a slave. John became very ill and had to beg for food. Eventually he was rescued and began his journey back home to his father in England.

This voyage, however, changed his life. He began to wrestle with his conscience during a violent storm in March 1748. After he had seen a shipmate washed overboard, a plea rose from within him: 'Lord, have mercy on us!' As he shouted, he wondered: could there be any mercy for one who blasphemed God's name as he had?

John Newton was led back to the Bible. On 21 March, lashed to the helm of a foundering ship, he considered Bible passages. He was especially struck by the story of the prodigal son in Luke chapter 15. He marvelled at the father who raced to meet his returning boy and he felt hope for his own life. When the badly damaged ship finally arrived back in harbour, a transformed John Newton went ashore.

He was 39. His mother's prayers were answered and John Newton was ordained a minister in the church. In the next few years, John wrote many hymns, but the most famous of all was 'Amazing Grace', a hymn based on his own testimony, and on the story of the prodigal son:

Amazing grace! (how sweet the sound)
That sav'd a wretch like me!
I once was lost, but now am found,
Was blind, but now I see.

John remained a faithful servant of God until his death on 21 December 1807. The epitaph he wrote for his tombstone reads:

John Newton, Clerk, once an infidel and libertine, a servant of slaves in Africa, was, by the rich mercy of our Lord and Saviour, Jesus Christ, restored, pardoned, and appointed to preach the Gospel he had long laboured to destroy.

What will be said about you? Maybe it's time to experience the Father's embrace. If you sense that it is, here's a great prayer of St Fursey:

> The arms of God be around my shoulders,
> The touch of the Holy Spirit upon my head,
> The sign of Christ's cross upon my forehead,
> The sound of the Holy Spirit in my ears,
> The fragrance of the Holy Spirit in my nostrils,
> The vision of heaven's company in my eyes,
> The conversation of heaven's company on my lips,
> The work of God's church in my hands,
> The service of God and the neighbour in my feet,
> A home for God in my heart,
> And to God, the Father of all, my entire being.
> Amen.

THE LOVESICK FATHER

PHILIP YANCEY

A young girl grows up on a cherry orchard just above Traverse City, Michigan. Her parents, a bit old-fashioned, tend to overreact to her nose ring, the music she listens to and the length of her skirts. They ground her a few times, and she seethes inside. 'I hate you!' she screams at her father when he knocks on the door of her room after an argument, and that night she acts on a plan she has mentally rehearsed scores of times. She runs away.

She has visited Detroit only once before, on a bus trip with her church youth group to watch the Tigers play. Because newspapers in Traverse City report in lurid detail the gangs, the drugs and the violence in downtown Detroit, she concludes that is probably the last place her parents will look for her. California, maybe, or Florida, but not Detroit.

Her second day there she meets a man who drives the biggest car she's ever seen. He offers her a ride, buys her lunch, arranges a place for her to stay. He gives her some pills that make her feel better than she's ever felt before. She was right all along, she decides: her parents were keeping her from all the fun.

The good life continues for a month, two months, a year. The man with the big car – she calls him 'Boss' – teaches her a few things that men like. Since she's under-age, men pay a premium for her. She lives in a penthouse, and orders room service whenever she wants. Occasionally she thinks about the folks back home, but their lives now seem so boring and provincial that she can hardly believe she grew up there.

She has a brief scare when she sees her picture printed on the back of a milk carton with the headline 'Have you seen this child?' But by now she has blonde hair, and with all the make-up and body-piercing jewellery she wears, nobody would mistake her for a child. Besides, most of her friends are runaways, and nobody squeals in Detroit.

After a year the first sallow signs of illness appear, and it amazes her how fast the boss turns mean. 'These days, we can't mess around,' he growls, and before she knows it she's out on the street without a penny to her name. She still turns a couple of tricks a night, but they don't pay much, and all the money goes to support her habit. When winter blows in she finds herself sleeping on metal grates outside the big department stores.

'Sleeping' is the wrong word – a teenage girl at night in downtown Detroit can never relax her guard. Dark bands circle her eyes. Her cough worsens.

One night as she lies awake listening for footsteps, all of a sudden everything about her life looks different. She no longer feels like a woman of the world. She feels like a little girl, lost in a cold and frightening city. She begins to whimper. Her pockets are empty and she's hungry. She needs a fix. She pulls her legs tight underneath her and shivers under the newspapers she's piled atop her coat. Something jolts a synapse of memory and a single image fills her mind: of May in Traverse City, when a million cherry trees bloom at once, with her golden retriever dashing through the rows and rows of blossomy trees in chase of a tennis ball.

God, why did I leave, she says to herself, and pain stabs at her heart. My dog back home eats better than I do now. She's sobbing, and she knows in a flash that more than anything else in the world she wants to go home.

Three straight phone calls, three straight connections with the answering machine. She hangs up without leaving a message the first two times, but the third time she says, 'Dad, Mom, it's me. I was wondering about maybe coming home. I'm catching a bus up your way, and it'll get there about midnight tomorrow. If you're not there, well, I guess I'll just stay on the bus until it hits Canada.'

It takes about seven hours for a bus to make all the stops between Detroit and Traverse City, and during that time she realizes the flaws in her plan. What if her parents are out of town and miss the message? Shouldn't she have waited another day or so until she could talk to them? And even if they are home, they probably wrote her off as dead long ago. She should have given them some time to overcome the shock.

Her thoughts bounce back and forth between those worries and the speech she is preparing for her father. 'Dad, I'm sorry. I know I was wrong. It's not your fault; it's all mine. Dad, can you forgive me?' She says the words over and over, her throat tightening even as she rehearses them. She hasn't apologized to anyone in years.

The bus has been driving with lights on since Bay City. Tiny snowflakes hit the road rubbed worn by thousands of tyres, and the asphalt steams. She's forgotten how dark it gets at night out here. A deer darts across the road and the bus swerves. Every so often, a billboard. A sign posting the mileage to Traverse City. Oh, God.

When the bus finally rolls into the station, its air brakes hissing in protest, the driver announces in a crackly voice over the microphone, 'Fifteen minutes, folks. That's all we have here.'

Fifteen minutes to decide her life. She checks herself in a compact mirror, smoothes her hair and licks the lipstick off her teeth. She looks at the tobacco stains on her fingertips, and wonders if her parents will notice. If they're there.

She walks into the terminal not knowing what to expect. Not one of the thousand scenes that have played out in her mind prepares her for what she sees. There, in the concrete-walls-and-plastic-chairs bus terminal in Traverse City, Michigan, stands a group of forty brothers and sisters and great-aunts and uncles and cousins and a grandmother and great-grandmother to boot. They're all wearing goofy party hats and blowing noise-makers, and taped across the entire wall of the terminal is a computer-generated banner that reads 'Welcome home!'

Out of the crowd of well-wishers breaks her dad. She stares out through the tears quivering in her eves like hot mercury and begins the memorized speech, 'Dad, I'm sorry. I know . . .'

He interrupts her. 'Hush, child. We've got no time for that. No time for apologies. You'll be late for the party. A banquet's waiting for you at home.'